THE PENTECOSTAL HERITAGE HYMNAL

EDITED BY
BISHOP CORNELIUS SHOWELL

Seymour Press *SP*
Lanham, MD

Copyright © 2022 Cornelius Showell

Copyright © 2022 Seymour Press

Scripture passages from the *King James Version Bible*, copyright©1989 by Thomas Nelson, Inc. Used by permission. All rights reserved.

Printed in the United States of America

Every effort has been made to trace the owner or holder of each copyright. If any rights have been inadvertently infringed upon, the Publishers ask that the omission be excused and agree to make the necessary corrections in subsequent editions.

ISBN: 978-1-938373-60-2
LCCN: 2022931533

***The Pentecostal Heritage Hymnal
is dedicated to***
Arnold Turpin
Rossie Grant
Andrew B. Collins
George Collins
Past and Present First Apostolic Faith Church
Musicians and Choir Members

Special Thanks
First Lady Augusta Showell
Vanderlyn E. Hampton
Lenora Merritt
Cornell Showell
H. Buddy Lakins Jr.
Walter S. Collins
Mary Smith

Content

Forward i
Preface iii
African American Hymnists and Composers v

Index of Hymns

Deeper, Deeper 1
His Name Should Be Praised 2
Jesus, the Son of God 4
All that Thrills My Soul 5
The Water Way 6
We'll Understand It Better By and By 8
The Day of Redemption 10
I Will Make the Darkness Light 11
The Storm Is Passing Over 12
The Solid Rock 13
Standing on the Promises 14
Saved, Saved 16
Rock of Ages 17
He Brought Me Out 18
Great Is Thy Faithfulness 20
How Great Thou Art 22
He Lives 24

If Jesus Goes With Me 26
All thru the Night 28
Blessed Assurance 29
The Lily of The Valley 30
I Heard the Voice of Jesus Say 32
The Cross Is Not Greater 33
There Is Power in the Blood 34
I See a Crimson Stream 35
Nothing But the Blood 36
When I See the Blood 37
Under The Blood 38
Thank God for the Blood 39
Washed in the Blood 40
Jesus Paid It All 41
There Is a Fountain Filled With Blood 42
At Calvary 43
The Blood Prevails 44
Hide You in the Blood 45
What a Wonderful Savior 46
There Shall Be Showers of Blessing 47
He Took My Sins Away 48
Christ Arose 49
Does Jesus Care? 50
God Will Take Care of You 51
Leave It There 52

Baptized into the Body	54
Friendship with Jesus	55
Come Unto Me	56
I've Anchored in Jesus	58
Jesus Breaks Every Fetter	59
The Beautiful Garden of Prayer	60
What a Friend We Have In Jesus	61
I Am Going On With Jesus	62
I Surrender All	63
No, Not One	64
Jesus Is Calling	65
Softly and Tenderly	66
Nothing Between	67
Is Thy Heart Right With God	68
Where He Leads Me	69
Jesus Is All the World to Me	70
Oh, How I Love Jesus	71
Is Your All on the Altar?	72
Whiter Than Snow	74
Draw Me Nearer	75
His Way With Thee	76
I Need Jesus	78
Fill Me Now	80
Face to Face	81
I'll Live On and On	82

I Love to Tell the Story	83
At the Cross	84
Look and Live	85
Seeking For Me	86
Sow Righteous Seed	87
Throw Out the Life-Line	88
Come, Thou Fount	89
Higher Ground	90
My Faith Looks Up To Thee	91
In Times Like These	92
His Yoke Is Easy	94
Just a Closer Walk with Thee	95
The Last Mile of the Way	96
Mountain Railroad	98
Beulah Land	99
All Hail the Power of Jesus' Name	100
A New Name in Glory	102
Where Jesus Is, 'Tis Heaven	104
O, That Will Be Glory	105
Oh, I Want to See Him	106
We Will Walk Thru the Streets of the City	108
We're Marching to Zion	109
Dwelling in Beulah Land	110
When We All Get to Heaven	112
Won't It Be Wonderful There	113

Just Over In Glory Land	114
When the Roll Is Called Up Yonder	116
One Day	118
Hold to God's Unchanging Hand	120
On Jordan's Stormy Banks	121
The Unclouded Day	122
It Pays to Serve Jesus	123
I Will Praise Him	124
I'd Rather Have Jesus	126
It Took a Miracle	128
Jesus Saves	129
My Father Watches Over Me	130
Jesus Is the Sweetest Name I Know	132
My Jesus, I Love Thee	133
Pass Me Not, O Gentle Savior	134
Somebody Saved Me	135
The Name of Jesus	136
Jesus, Lover of My Soul	137
Trust and Obey	138
Trusting Jesus	139
Leaving All Follow to Jesus	140
Count Your Blessing	141
Praise Thy Name	142
Glory to His Name	143
God is Great in My Soul	144

Come, Thou Almighty King	145
To God Be the Glory	146
Tis So Sweet to Trust in Jesus	147
By the Rivers of Babylon	148
Holiness Unto to the Lord	150
The Comforter Has Come	152
The Name of God	154
The Great I Am	156
All in Him	158
God Leads Us Along	160
Yesterday, Today, Forever	162
Yield Not to Temptation	162
I've Believed the True Report	164
Since the Comforter Came	166
Go on In Jesus Name	167
The Shepherd Calling His Sheep	168
Draw Me, Dear Jesus	170
Savior, Like a Shepherd Lead Us	171
Death Hath No Terror	172
More Abundantly	173
Worthy Is the Lamb	174
Do You Know Him	176
Let the Redeemed Say So	178
I'm Happy with Jesus Alone	180
Blessed Be the Name	181

Now I'm Saved	182
Your Heart Must Be Clean	183
Let Jesus Fix It For You	184
It Is Well With My Soul	185
Lead Me to Calvary	186
I Must Tell Jesus	187
Love Lifted Me	188
Revive Us Again	189
Just As I Am	190
Near the Cross	191
He was Nailed to the Cross	192
Kneel at the Cross	193
Come and Dine	194
The Haven of Rest	196
He Hideth My Soul	198
I Am Determined To Hold Out	200
He Leadeth Me	202
Blessed Quietness	203
Farther Along	204
A Glorious Church	205
Don't Turn the Savior Away	206
We Have an Anchor	207
Take the Name of Jesus with You	208
My Savior, First of All	209
More About Jesus	210

Footprints of Jesus 211
O Happy Day 213
I Walk With the King 214
Wonderful Peace 215
I Need Thee Every Hour 216
Jesus Understands 217
Jesus, Savior, Pilot Me 218
I Feel Like Traveling On 219
The Way of the Cross Leads Home 220
Sweeter as the Years Go By 221
In the Service of the King 223
All the Way My Savior Leads Me 224
Look to the Lamb of God 225
Alone 226
Woke Up This Morning with My Mind 227
Heavenly Sunlight 228
Are You Washed in the Blood? 229
Almost Persuaded 230
Guide Me, O Thou Great Jehovah 231
A Child of the King 232
Battle Hymn of the Republic 233
I Love Jesus Best of All 234
Even Me 235
Joy Unspeakable 237
Onward Christian Soldiers 238

His Eye Is on the Sparrow 239
That is Why I'm Going to Continue 241
I'm Going Through 243
Leaning on the Everlasting Arms 245
O Master, Let Me Walk with Thee 246
Master, the Tempest Is Raging 247
Never Alone 249
Joy to the World 251
O Come, All Ye Faithful 252
The Old Rugged Cross 253
When The Battle's Over 255
God Be With You 257
Since Jesus Came into My Heart 258
Give Me a Clean Heart 259
The Author and Finisher 261
Sweet Hour of Prayer 262
Just a Little Talk with Jesus 263
All Alone 264
Answer Him Lord I Will 265
Jesus, I'll Never Forget 266
I'm Saved 267
There's A Highway to Heaven 268
He Never Has Left Me Alone 269
Caught Up to Meet Him 270
I'm Going Back to Jesus 271

You Shall Wear a Golden Crown 272
Oh, the Joy That Came To Me 273
I Was Lost 274
Going On All I Know 275
Oh, What's He Done For Me 276
Never Draw Back 277
Yes, There Is Power in His Name 278
I Can Tell the World About This 279
Nobody but You Lord 280
Is Everybody Happy? 281
I'm Going to Live the Life I Sing About 282
Let's Go Back 283
I Am Out on the Battlefield 284
He's Got the Whole World in His Hand 285
What He Done for Me 286
Come and Go With Me 287
Walk With Me Lord, Walk With Me 288
I Will To Know 288
I Love Jesus 289
Come By Here Good Lord, Come By Here 289
There Is Something Mighty Sweet 290
I'm So Glad Jesus Lifted Me 290
I'm Pressing on All I Know 291
If I Were You, I'd Make A Change 291
It Is Truly Wonderful 292

Scripture Readings 293
Index of Topics 375
Index of First Lines 387
Index of Authors and Composers 395

FORWARD

It is a privilege to write this forward for the historical worship and Praise hymnal. Apostle Cornelius Showell's connection to the Apostolic Pentecostal tradition extends to the Azusa Street revival in 1906, his late great uncle Bishop Joseph M. Turpin, and his father, Bishop Winfield Amos Showell. In addition, their wives and children have contributed to the great legacy passed on to this generation.

I can think of several ways to preserve our heritage, but none more significantly than collecting the "psalms, hymns, and spiritual songs" produced by those early pioneers. These songs of worship and praise are scripturally grounded. They bear witness to the theology of the Pentecostal church and the confidence that its witness was on the right side of the move God in the 20th Century. Our spiritual parents drew upon the hymns and spiritual songs of other traditions in the Christian Faith that corroborated their vision and hope and sustained them in their quest for holiness and righteous living. This volume does the same.

May this volume of worship and praise songs nurture the souls and faith of believers. May these songs refresh our commitment to the great legacy that was passed on to us, and may they challenge and inspire us to continue the great spirit of worship and praise to God in the name of our Lord and Savior, Jesus the Christ. Congratulations to Apostle Cornelius F. Showell for your outstanding work on this sacred project

Apostle James I. Clark, Jr., Ed. D.
Church of Our Lord Jesus Christ,
Presiding Bishop

PREFACE

Music has played an integral part in the worship of black Holiness-Pentecostals. Hymns, spirituals, and gospel choruses have always expressed important theological and biblical concepts regarding God, Christology, salvation, sanctification, Spirit baptism, and holiness. They have been used in personal testimony, as teaching tools, to celebrate special occasions, and in the observance of the sacraments. The Pentecostal Heritage Hymnal was conceived to preserve the tradition of great music that has been foundational for past generations of sanctified folks and should remain an important center of contemporary Pentecostal worship.

> *Speaking to yourselves in psalms and hymns and spiritual songs, singing and making melody in your heart to the Lord* (Eph. 5:19)

AFRICAN AMERICAN HYMNISTS AND COMPOSERS

Charles Albert Tindley, "the grandfather of Gospel Music," was born in 1851 in Berlin, Maryland, to former slaves. He moved to Philadelphia and found employment as a janitor at the Calvary Methodist Episcopal Church. Tindley attended night classes and correspondence courses at Boston University.

Ordained a Methodist minister, he became the pastor of the Calvary Methodist Episcopal Church, the church that first employed him as a janitor. The congregation grew to over 7,000 and was later renamed Tindley Temple Methodist Church.

Tindley published five hymnals, including *Nothing Between My Soul* and *My Savior, When the Storms of Life Are Raging, If the World from You Withhold, Beams of Heaven As I Go*, and *We Are Tossed and Driven.* In 1902, he wrote I'll Overcome Someday," the hymn was later arranged into the Civil Rights freedom song, "We Shall Overcome." His compositions such as The Storm Is Passing Over, The Lord Will Make A Way Somehow, and We'll Understand It Better By and By conveyed Christian believers' struggles, sufferings, and deliverance.

**Charles Price Jones** was born in Rome, Georgia, in 1865. He accepted the doctrine of Holiness and sanctification in 1894. Jones and fellow Baptist minister Charles H. Mason formed the holiness organization, Church of God in Christ, in 1897 in Jackson, Mississippi.

However, Jones disassociated himself after Mason converted to Pentecostalism. He and his non-Pentecostal followers organized the Church of Christ (Holiness) U.S.A. in 1907. He served as the elected bishop of the organization from 1928 until his death in 1949.

Jones authored over a thousand hymns and published three Church of Christ (Holiness) hymnals, *Jesus Only* in 1899, *Jesus Only Nos. 1 and 2* in 1901, and *His Fullness* in 1906. Many of his hymns became standards of the Holiness and Pentecostal movement. His most noted works are Deeper, Deeper," Come Unto Me," and "I Will Make the Darkness Light."

**Garfield Thomas Haywood** was born in Greencastle, Indiana, in 1880. He joined the Apostolic Faith Assembly in 1908. In 1909, Haywood succeeded Henry Prentiss as the Apostolic Faith Assembly pastor. The membership had grown from thirteen to fifty members within a few years. Later renamed Christ Temple, the church became one of the largest interracial congregations in the United States.

In 1915, Haywood embraced baptism in Jesus' Name and joined the Oneness movement. He was highly instrumental in spreading Oneness Pentecostal through his monthly periodical, *A Voice in the Wilderness*. In 1925, Haywood became the first presiding bishop of the Pentecostal Assemblies of the World and served until 1931.

Haywood published his first hymnal, *The Bridegroom Songs,* in 1919. A prolific writer, he penned over nineteen hymns, including "Jesus, the Son of God," "I See a Crimson Stream," "The Day of Redemption," and "Thank God for the Blood." His songs appealed to both Trinitarian and Oneness Pentecostals.

**Thoro Harris** was born on March 31, 1874, in Washington DC. His father was African American, and his mother was German. A child prodigy, Harris began taking piano lessons at the age of five, but it was not until he entered Battle Creek College at the age of fifteen that he became skilled at different musical techniques. In 1902, he moved to Boston and published his first hymnal, *Echoes of Paradise*. Harris then relocated to Chicago, Illinois, where he opened the Windsor Music Company in 1903.

In 1914, he wrote: "Baptized in Jesus' Name" after embracing the apostolic doctrine. Though he was never Baptist, in 1925, he edited The New Hymnal, the first collection of Swedish-American Baptist hymns published in English (and containing thirty-nine of his songs). Harris moved to Eureka Springs, Arkansas, in 1932 and remained there until his death in 1955.

The multi-talented Harris composed and arranged over two hundred hymns. He published four Pentecostal hymnals, *The Blessed Hope* (1910), *Jesus is Coming Soon* (1914), *Songs of His Coming* (1919), and *Songs We Love* (1921). His hymnals featured other black hymn-writers such as G. T. Haywood, Charles P. Jones, and A. R. Schooler. Harris' most celebrated work, "All That Thrills My Soul is Jesus," is a favorite among Pentecostals and non-Pentecostals.

**Robert Clarence Lawson,** the founder of the Church of Our Lord Jesus Christ of the Apostolic Faith, was born in New Iberia, Louisiana, in 1883. He was miraculously healed of tuberculosis and filled with the Holy Spirit under the leadership of G. T. Haywood. He joined Pentecostal Assemblies of the World in 1914 and pastored the Apostolic Faith Assembly in Columbus, Ohio. In addition, Lawson planted PAW churches in San Antonio, Texas, and St. Louis, Missouri. under the title "Church of Christ of the Apostolic Faith."

One of the early black leaders of PAW, Lawson served as a field superintendent and on the General Board of Elders. In 1919, he resigned over the issue of divorce and remarriage. He traveled to Harlem, New York City, and founded Refuge Church of Christ. His organization was incorporated under the name Church of Our Lord Jesus Christ of the Apostolic Faith in 1931.

He published the *Songs of Christ* hymnal in 1924, which included 100 compositions written by various Oneness Pentecostals such as G. T. Haywood, Ora Wald, Esther Pinn Richardson, Hattie Pryor, and A. R. Schooler. Lawson's hymns, "His Name Should Be Praised," "Let the Redeemed Say So," and "God is Great in My Soul." became popular songs of praise among Black Apostolic.

**Sobrina Kathleen Grimes** (S. K. Grimes), missionary and the wife of Samuel Joshua Grimes, the second presiding bishop of Pentecostal Assemblies of the World, was born in Canada but migrated to New York in 1910. She met Samuel while attending the National Bible Institute in Philadelphia in 1917. The couple worked as PAW missionaries in Liberia, West Africa, from 1920 to 1924. Unfortunately, she contracted malaria, which afflicted her for the remainder of her life.

She served as the first lady of PAW from 1932 to 1967 and was instrumental in organizing the Women's auxiliary. Grimes and her husband also sponsored the education of Ellen Moore Hopkins, a nursing student from Liberia, West Africa. In 1946, Hopkins established the Samuel Grimes Maternity and Welfare Center in Kakola, Liberia. The center assisted hundreds of orphans and trained nurses in Liberia.

An accomplished musician and songwriter, Grimes published an eight-song compilation entitled, *Echoes of Zion* in 1924. The hymnal featured "The Great I Am" and her testimony of receiving the baptism of the Holy Spirit, "Since the Comforter Came."

 **Alexander Robinson (A. R.) Schooler,** one of the original bishops of the Pentecostals Assemblies of the World, was born in Lancaster, Kentucky. He organized the Pentecostal Church of Christ in Cleveland, Ohio, and served as pastor until 1915. He later moved to Chicago, Illinois, and established the Apostolic Faith Church.

Within PAW, Schooler served as one of the four early black field superintendents. He founded the Ohio District Council and worked with Joseph M. Turpin in forming the Eastern District Council. In 1919 Schooler was elected Vice General Chairperson and appointed Executive Vice-Chair, a post he held until 1922. He was elected to the office of bishop after the body was reorganized under an episcopal system of leadership. Schooler left PAW and joined the Church of God in Jesus Christ (Apostolic), founded by Randolph A. Carr.

Schooler co-wrote several hymns with his close friend Thoro Harris, who lived in Chicago, Illinois. He wrote very distinct apostolic hymns such as "The Name," "God Died for Me," and "The Author and the Finisher."

 **Gladstone Thomas Harewood** was born in St. Lucia, West Indies, in 1898. His family immigrated to the United States while Gladstone was a young boy in 1908. His uncle, Fitzherbert Pilgrim, raised him in Chicago. Gladstone's brother, Richard, became the first black to win statewide public office in Illinois. He later served as a judge in the Circuit Court of Cook County.

He joined the Apostolic Faith Church, founded by A. R. Schooler in Chicago, and served as assistant pastor. Harewood took over the leadership of a small mission once led by Theodore Sherriff in 1928. He lived in several other Midwestern states—Indiana, Wisconsin, and Iowa before settling in Los Angeles, California, where he led a congregation until he died in 1985.

Harewood wrote over a hundred songs. Unfortunately, many were mistakenly credited to G. T. Haywood, songwriter and the first presiding bishop of PAW. His most popular songs include "The Blood Prevails," "I Love Jesus Best of All," "Draw Me, Dear Jesus," and "Now I'm Saved."

His Name Should Be Praised

Jesus, the Son of God

1. Do you know Jesus, Our Lord, our Savior, Jesus the Son of God? Have you ever seen Him, Or shared of His favor? Jesus the Son of God.
2. God gave Him a ransom Our souls to recover, Jesus the Son of God. His blood made us worthy His Spirit to hover, Jesus the Son of God.
3. O who would reject Him, Despise, or forsake Him, Jesus the Son of God? O who ever sought Him, And He would not take Him? Jesus the Son of God.
4. Then some day from heaven, On clouds of bright glory, Jesus the Son of God. Will come for His jewels, Most precious and holy, Jesus the Son of God.

CHORUS

O sweet Wonder! O sweet Wonder! Jesus the Son of God; How I adore Thee! O how I love Thee! Jesus the Son of God.

Words and Music: G. T. Haywood, 1914

Words and Music: Hattie E. Pryor, 1919

We'll Understand It Better By and By

Words and Music: Charles A. Tindley
Arr. F. A. Clark

The Storm Is Passing Over

1. O courage, my soul, and let us journey on, For though the night is dark, it won't be very long. O thanks be to God, the morning light appears, And the storm is passing over, Hallelujah!
2. O billows rolling high, and thunder shakes the ground, The lightnings flash, and tempest all around, But Jesus walks the sea and calms the angry waves, And the storm is passing over, Hallelujah!
3. The stars have disappeared, and distant lights are dim, My soul is filled with fears, the seas are breaking in. I hear the Master cry, "Be not afraid, 'tis I," And the storm is passing over, Hallelujah!
4. Now soon we shall reach the distant shining shore, Then free from all the storms, we'll rest forevermore. And safe within the veil, we'll furl the riven sail, And the storm will all be over, Hallelujah!

CHORUS
Hallelujah! Hallelujah! The storm is passing over, Hallelujah!

Words and Music: Charles A. Tindley, 1905

15

Russell K. Carter, 1886

Saved, Saved

He Brought Me Out

1. My heart was distressed 'neath Jehovah's dread frown, And low in the pit where my sins dragged me down; I cried to the Lord from the deep miry clay, Who tenderly brought me out to golden day.

2. He placed me upon the strong Rock by His side, My steps were established and here I'll abide; No danger of falling while here I remain, But stand by His grace until the crown I gain.

3. He gave me a song, 'twas a new song of praise; By day and by night its sweet notes I will raise; My heart's overflowing, I'm happy and free; I'll praise my Redeemer, Who has rescued me.

4. I'll sing of His wonderful mercy to me, I'll praise Him till all men His goodness shall see; I'll sing of salvation at home and abroad, Till many shall hear the truth and trust in God.

Words: Henry J. Zelley, 1898
Music: Henry L. Gilmour

Great Is Thy Faithfulness

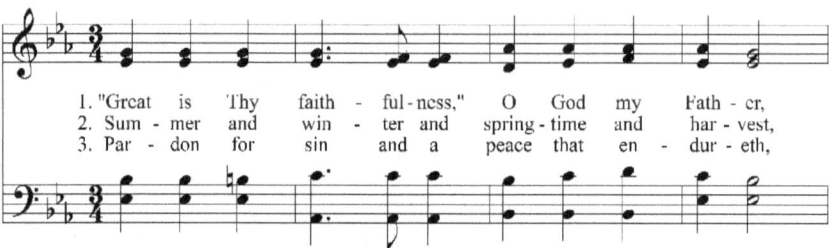

1. "Great is Thy faith-ful-ness," O God my Fath-er,
2. Sum-mer and win-ter and spring-time and har-vest,
3. Par-don for sin and a peace that en-dur-eth,

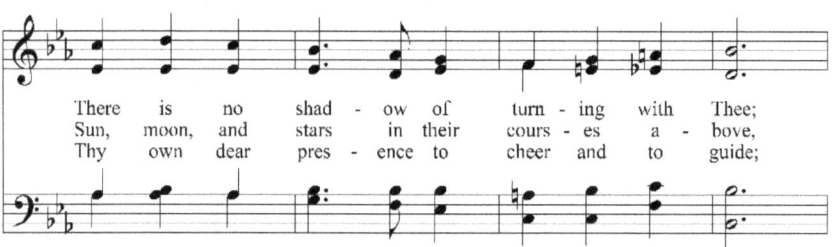

There is no shad-ow of turn-ing with Thee;
Sun, moon, and stars in their cours-es a-bove,
Thy own dear pres-ence to cheer and to guide;

Thou chang-est not, Thy com-pas-sions, they fail not;
Join with all na-ture in man-i-fold wit-ness,
Strength for to-day and bright hope for to-mor-row,

As Thou hast been Thou for-ev-er wilt be.
To Thy great faith-ful-ness, mer-cy, and love.
Bless-ings all mine, with ten thou-sand be-side!

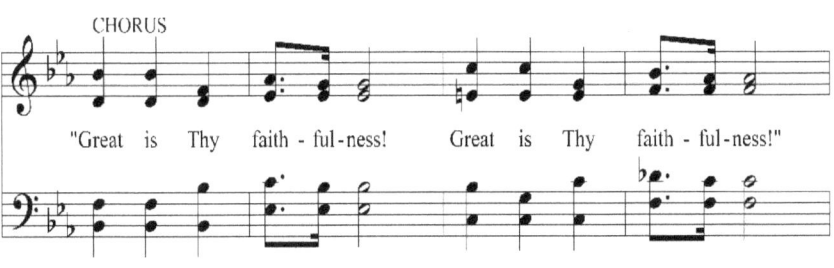

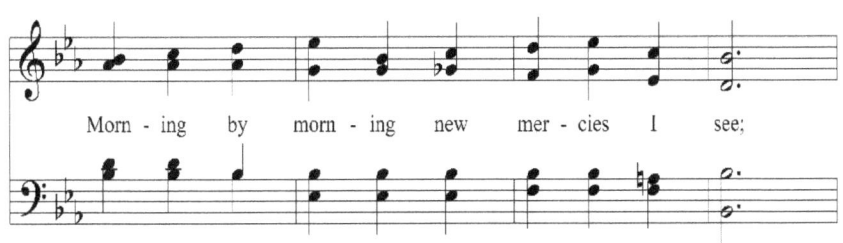

Words: Thomas O. Chisholm, 1923

How Great Thou Art

1. O Lord my God! When I in awesome wonder
2. When through the woods and forest glades I wander
3. And when I think that God, His Son not sparing,
4. When Christ shall come with shout of acclamation

Consider all the worlds Thy hands have made,
And hear the birds sing sweetly in the trees;
Sent Him to die, I scarce can take it in;
And take me home, what joy shall fill my heart!

I see the stars, I hear the rolling
When I look down from lofty mountain
That on the cross my burden gladly
Then I shall bow in humble ado-

Words and Music: Carl Boberg, © 1986 Lillenas Publishing Company

He Lives

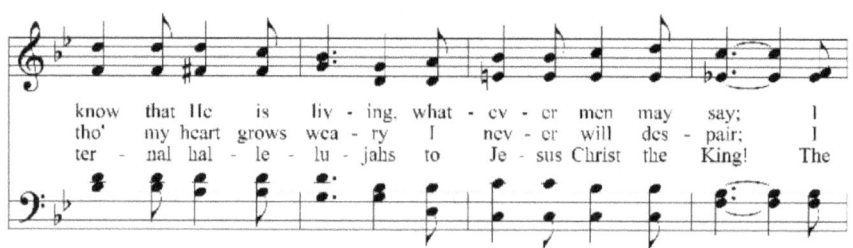

Words and Music: Alfred H. Ackley

27

Words and Music: C. Austin Miles, 1908

All Thru the Night

1. Jesus Christ my Lord will keep me All thru the night.
2. Darker grow the shadows 'round me, Dark is the night.
3. Hark! A solemn voice is sounding All thru the night.
4. Sun of righteousness appearing, He'll end the night.

By His counsel guide and lead me, All thru the night.
Snares of Satan oft surround me, Dark is the night.
'Tis the voice of God resounding All thru the night.
I can see the day is nearing When ends the night.

Night of sin and death and sorrow; He will keep till dawns the morrow;
But my pathway Jesus brightens, Ev'ry heavy burden lightens;
Telling of the preparation Needed by earth's ev'ry nation
Sleeping saints will rise all glorious, Raptured, too, will swell the chorus;

From this world I need not borrow, All thru the night.
Nothing moves me, nothing frightens, Tho' dark the night.
To escape the tribulation, Earth's darkest night.
Earth will crown my King victorious, Thus ends the night.

Words and Music: Melvia Booker, 1918

The Lily of the Valley

1. I have found a friend in Je-sus, He's ev-'ry-thing to me, He's the
2. He all my grief has tak-en, and all my sor-rows borne; In temp-
3. He will nev-er, nev-er leave me, nor yet for-sake me here, While I

fair - est of ten thou - sand to my soul; The
ta - tion He's my strong and might - y tow'r; I have
live by faith and do His bless - ed will; A

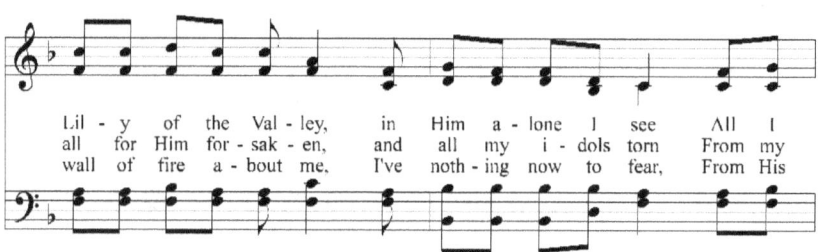

Lil - y of the Val - ley, in Him a - lone I see All I
all for Him for - sak - en, and all my i - dols torn From my
wall of fire a - bout me, I've noth - ing now to fear, From His

need to cleanse and make me ful - ly whole. In
heart and now He keeps me by His pow'r. Though
man - na He my hun - gry soul shall fill. Then

Words: Charles W. Fry, 1881
Music: William S. Hays

I Heard the Voice of Jesus Say

1. I heard the voice of Jesus say, "Come unto Me and rest;
Lay down, thou weary one, lay down Thy head upon My breast."
I came to Jesus as I was, Weary and worn, and sad;
I found in Him a resting place, And He has made me glad.

2. I heard the voice of Jesus say, "Behold, I freely give
The living water; thirsty one, Stoop down, and drink, and live."
I came to Jesus, and I drank Of that life-giving stream;
My thirst was quench'd, my soul revived, And now I live in Him.

3. I heard the voice of Jesus say, "I am this dark world's Light
Look unto Me, thy morn shall rise, And all thy day be bright."
I looked to Jesus, and I found In Him my Star, my Sun;
And in that Light of life I'll walk, Till trav'ling days are done.

Words: Horatius Bonar, 1846

There Is Power in the Blood

Words and Music: Lewis E. Jones, 1899

I See a Crimson Stream

1. On Calv-'ry's hill of sor-row Where sin's de-mands were paid,
2. To-day no con-dem-na-tion A-bides to turn a-way
3. When gloom and sad-ness whis-per You've sin'd no use to pray,
4. And when we reach the por-tal Where life for-ev-er reigns,

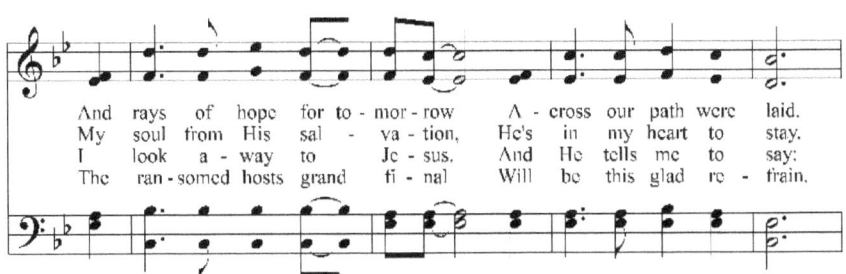

And rays of hope for to-mor-row A-cross our path were laid.
My soul from His sal-va-tion, He's in my heart to stay.
I look a-way to Je-sus. And He tells me to say;
The ran-somed hosts grand fi-nal Will be this glad re-frain.

CHORUS

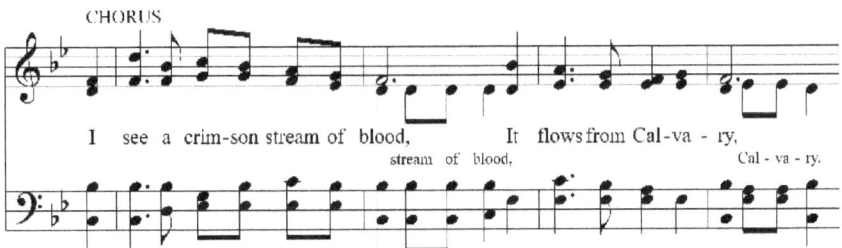

I see a crim-son stream of blood, It flows from Cal-va-ry,
              stream of blood,   Cal-va-ry.

Its waves which reach the throne of God, Are sweep-ing o-ver me.
              throne of God,   o-ver me.

Words and Music: G. T. Haywood, 1920

Nothing but the Blood

1. What can wash away my sin? Nothing but the blood of Jesus;
2. For my pardon, this I see, Nothing but the blood of Jesus;
3. Nothing can for sin atone, Nothing but the blood of Jesus;
4. This is all my hope and peace, Nothing but the blood of Jesus;
5. Now by this I'll o-ver-come Nothing but the blood of Jesus;
6. Glory! Glory! This I sing Nothing but the blood of Jesus;

What can make me whole again? Nothing but the blood of Jesus.
For my cleansing this my plea, Nothing but the blood of Jesus.
Naught of good that I have done, Nothing but the blood of Jesus.
This is all my right-cous-ness, Nothing but the blood of Jesus.
Now by this I'll reach my home Nothing but the blood of Jesus.
All my praise for this I bring Nothing but the blood of Jesus.

CHORUS

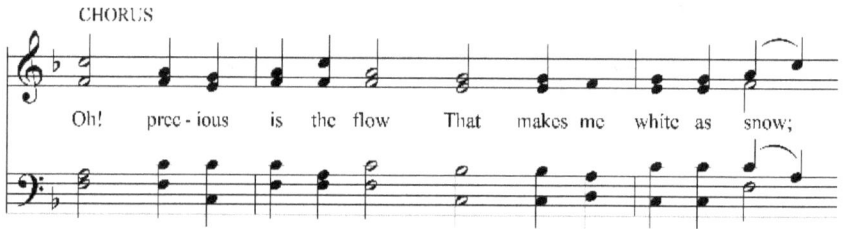

Oh! precious is the flow That makes me white as snow;

No other fount I know, Nothing but the blood of Jesus.

Words and Music: Robert Lowry, 1876

Words and Music: John G. Foote, 19th Century

Under the Blood

1. Lord, keep my soul from day to day, Under the blood, under the blood;
2. The sinner's refuge here alone, Under the blood, under the blood;
3. Lord, with Thyself my spirit fill, Under the blood, under the blood;
4. Sweet peace abides within the heart, Under the blood, under the blood;
5. The Holy Spirit, hour by hour, Under the blood, under the blood;

Take doubt and fear and sin away, Under the precious blood.
Here Jesus makes salvation known, Under the precious blood.
And work in me to do Thy will, Under the precious blood.
And gifts divine their joy impart, Under the precious blood.
Exerts His sanctifying pow'r, Under the precious blood.

CHORUS
Under the blood, the precious blood, Under the cleansing, healing flood;
Keep me, Savior, from day to day, Under the precious blood.

Words: Eliza E. Hewitt, 1851 - 1920

Thank God for the Blood

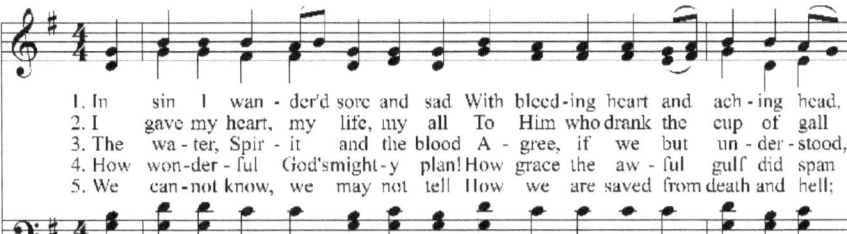

1. In sin I wan-der'd sore and sad With bleed-ing heart and ach-ing head,
2. I gave my heart, my life, my all To Him who drank the cup of gall
3. The wa-ter, Spir-it and the blood A-gree, if we but un-der-stood,
4. How won-der-ful God's might-y plan! How grace the aw-ful gulf did span
5. We can-not know, we may not tell How we are saved from death and hell;

Till Je-sus came and sweet-ly said, "I'll take thy sins a-way."
To raise the guilt-y from the fall And take their sins a-way.
In mak-ing sin-ners pure and good, And take our sins a-way.
When He took on the form of man To take our sins a-way.
Thru faith we know that all is well; He took our sins a-way.

CHORUS

Thank God for the blood! Thank God for the blood!
Thank God for the cleans-ing blood! Thank God for the crim-son flood!

Thank God for the blood That wash-es white as snow.
Thank God for the Sav-ior's blood

Words and Music: G. T. Haywood, 1919

40

Washed in the Blood

1. Washed in the blood, by the Spirit sealed, Christ in His word is to me revealed; Glory to God! in my soul doth shine God, my salvation, and His life is mine!
2. Once I was blind, but behold I see; God from above now hath shined into me; Cleansed from all sin, in His word I behold Wealth which can never be compared to gold.
3. O that the world might the Saviour see, That blessed Saviour who saved poor me! O how the lost ones would come shouting home, Never, never, never, nevermore to roam!
4. Washed in the blood! Sinner, come today; Jesus so freely the debt will pay; Come to His arms, to His arms of grace, Come, now in meekness, seek the Saviour's face.

CHORUS
Washed in the blood, washed in the blood! Washed in the blood, in the soul-cleansing blood! Sealed in the Spirit true, and washed in the blood!
O glory! Hallelujah! O glory!

Words and Music: Charles P. Jones

Jesus Paid It All

1. I hear the Sav-ior say, "Thy strength in-deed is small; Child of weak-ness, watch and pray, Find in Me thine all in all."
2. For noth-ing good have I Where-by Thy grace to claim; I'll wash my gar-ments white In the blood of Cal-v'ry's Lamb.
3. And now com-plete in Him, My robe, His right-eous-ness, Close shel-tered 'neath His side, I am di-vine-ly blest.
4. Lord, now in-deed I find Thy pow'r, and Thine a-lone, Can change the lep-er's spots And melt the heart of stone.
5. When from my dy-ing bed My ran-somed soul shall rise, "Je-sus died my soul to save," Shall rend the vault-ed skies.
6. And when be-fore the throne I stand in Him com-plete, I'll lay my tro-phies down, All down at Je-sus' feet.

CHORUS
Je - sus paid it all, All to Him I owe; Sin had left a crim-son stain, He washed it white as snow.

Words: Elvina M. Hall, 1865

44

The Blood Prevails

1. I rejoice in my Savior's love to-day, For His pow'r has set me free I am happy in Jesus, for this I can say, The precious blood prevails.
2. Tho the world with its vanities has tried, To prevent my progress here; I am trusting to-day in that crimson tide, In Jesus I will abide;
3. Now the fountain is open in David's house For a world's unrighteousness; Life and healing and cleansing may be yours to-day If you will His word obey.
4. Tho your sins be as scarlet He'll make them like wool, If as crimson He'll make them like snow; He is longing to grant you a place in His fold And give you His joy untold.

CHORUS
O the blood prevails, the blood of our blessed Lord, Its pow'r to save is just as in olden days; The blood prevails, no matter how foes assail; Thank God, the blood prevails.

Words and Music: Gladstone T. Harewood, 1928

Hide You In the Blood

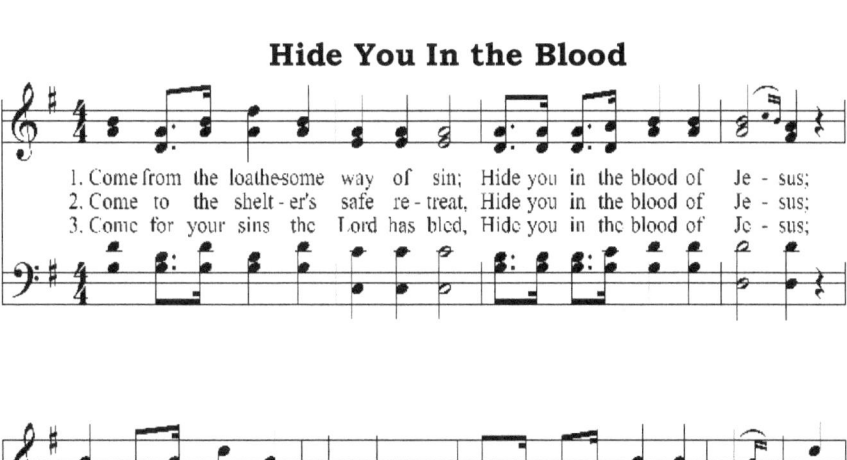

1. Come from the loathesome way of sin; Hide you in the blood of Je - sus;
2. Come to the shelt-er's safe re-treat, Hide you in the blood of Je - sus;
3. Come for your sins the Lord has bled, Hide you in the blood of Je - sus;

Come for the Lord will take you in, Hide you in the blood of Je - sus. O
Come for the storms a - round you beat, Hide you in the blood of Je - sus.
Come tho' they be like crim - son red, Hide you in the blood of Je - sus.

CHORUS

hide you in the blood, For the storms are rag-ing high, O
O hide in the blood. For the storms rag - ing high,

hide you in the blood, Till the dan - gers pass you by.
O hide

Words and Music: Hampton H. Sew

There Shall Be Showers of Blessing

1. "There shall be show-ers of bless-ing": This is the prom-ise of love:
2. "There shall be show-ers of bless-ing"— Prec-ious re-viv-ing a-gain:
3. "There shall be show-ers of bless-ing": Send them up-on us, O Lord;
4. "There shall be show-ers of bless-ing": Oh, that to-day they might fall,

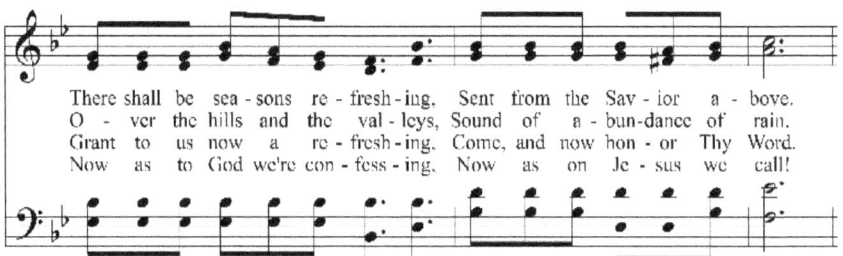

There shall be sea-sons re-fresh-ing, Sent from the Sav-ior a-bove.
O-ver the hills and the val-leys, Sound of a-bun-dance of rain.
Grant to us now a re-fresh-ing, Come, and now hon-or Thy Word.
Now as to God we're con-fess-ing, Now as on Je-sus we call!

CHORUS

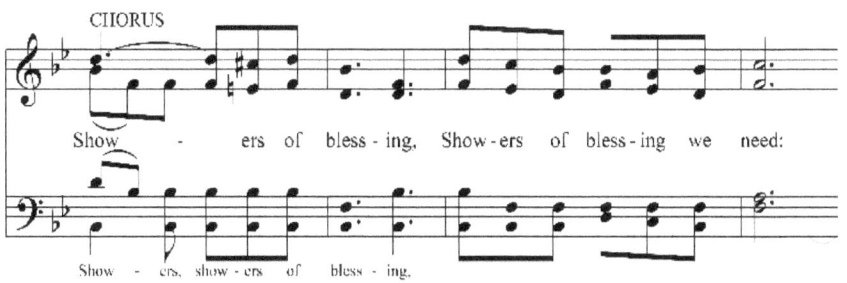

Show - ers of bless-ing, Show-ers of bless-ing we need;
Show - ers, show-ers of bless-ing,

Mer-cy-drops round us are fall-ing, But for the show-ers we plead.

Words: Daniel W. Whittle, 1883

Christ Arose

1. Low in the grave He lay; Jesus my Savior! Waiting the coming day;
2. Vainly they watch His bed; Jesus my Savior! Vainly they seal the dead;
3. Death cannot keep his prey; Jesus my Savior! He tore the bars away;

Jesus my Lord! Up from the grave He arose, With a mighty triumph o'er His foes; He arose a Victor from the dark domain, And He lives forever with His saints to reign. He arose! He arose! Hallelujah! Christ arose!

Words and Music: Robert Lowry, 1874

Does Jesus Care

50

1. Does Jesus care when my heart is pained Too deeply for mirth or song; As the burdens press, And the cares distress, And the way grows weary and long?

2. Does Jesus care when my way is dark With a nameless dread and fear? As the daylight fades Into deep night shades, Does He care enough to be near?

3. Does Jesus care when I've tried and failed To resist some temptation strong; When for my deep grief There is no relief, Tho' my tears flow all the night long?

4. Does Jesus care when I've said "good-bye" To the dearest on earth to me, And my sad heart aches Till it nearly breaks, Is it aught to Him? Does He see?

CHORUS

O yes, He cares, I know He cares, His heart is touched with my grief; When the days are weary, The long night dreary, I know my Savior cares.

Words: Frank E. Graeff

Leave It There

Words and Music: Charles A. Tindley, 1916

54

Baptized into the Body

1. Have you been bap-tized in-to the Bod-y? Bap-tized with the Ho-ly Ghost; There is but one way to en-ter in it, Just as they did on Pen-te-cost.

2. There is but one Church, Bride or Bod-y, And in-to it we're all bap-tized; By the one, true, prom-ised Ho-ly Spir-it; Tho' by the world we're all de-spised.

3. Ev-'ry creed has claim'd to be the Bod-y, But the "plumb-line" proved un-true; All their dreams, for God has so de-ter-mined, To bring His Son's true Bride to view.

CHORUS
Are you in the Church tri-um-phant? Are you in the Sav-ior's Bride? Come and be bap-tized in-to the Bod-y, And for-ev-er-more a-bide.

4. Many thought that they were in the Body,
'Til the Holy Ghost had come;
When the Word of God was opened to them,
They entered in, and yet there's room.

5. Those who died before the Holy Spirit
Came upon us from on high
May, by faith with Saints of old departed,
Arise to meet Him in the sky.

6. When the Bridegroom comes, will you be ready?
And your vessel all filled and bright?
You will be among the foolish virgins
If you do not walk in the light.

Words and Music: G. T. Haywood, 1914

Friendship with Jesus

1. A friend of Jesus! Oh, what bliss That one so weak as I
Should ev-er have a Friend like this To lead me to the sky!
2. A Friend when oth-er friend-ships cease, A Friend when oth-ers fail,
A Friend who gives me joy and peace, A Friend when foes as-sail!
3. A Friend when sick-ness lay me low, A Friend when death draws near,
A Friend as through the vale I go, A Friend to help and cheer!
4. A Friend when life's short race is o'er A Friend when earth is past,
A Friend to meet on Heav-en's shore, A Friend when home at last!

CHORUS

Friend-ship with Je-sus! Fel-low-ship di-vine!
Oh, what bless-ed, sweet com-mun-ion! Je-sus is a Friend of mine.

Words: Joseph C. Ludgate, 1898

Come Unto Me

1. Hear the blessed Savior calling the oppressed,
"Oh, ye heavy-laden, come to Me and rest;
Come, no longer tarry, I your load will bear,
Bring Me every burden, bring Me every care."

2. Are you disappointed, wan-d'ring here and there,
Dragging chains of doubt and loaded down with care?
Do unholy feelings struggle in your breast?
Bring your case to Jesus, He will give you rest.

3. Stumbling on the mountains dark with sin and shame,
Stumbling toward the pit of hell's consuming flame;
By the pow'rs of sin deluded and oppressed,
Hear the tender Shepherd, "Come to Me and rest."

4. Have you by temptation often conquered been,
Has a sense of weakness brought distress within?
Christ will sanctify you, if you'll claim His best;
In the Holy Spirit, He will give you rest.

Words and Music: C. P. Jones, © 1965, renewed 1993 Lillenas Publishing Company

I've Anchored in Jesus

1. Up-on life's bound-less o-cean where might-y bil-lows roll, I've fixed my
2. He keeps my soul from e-vil and gives me bless-ed peace, His voice hath
3. He is my Friend and Sav-ior, in Him my an-chor's cast, He drives a-

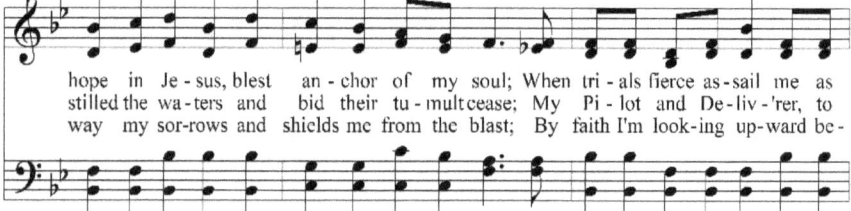

hope in Je-sus, blest an-chor of my soul; When tri-als fierce as-sail me as
stilled the wa-ters and bid their tu-mult cease; My Pi-lot and De-liv-'rer, to
way my sor-rows and shields me from the blast; By faith I'm look-ing up-ward be-

storms are gath-'ring o'er, I rest up-on His mer-cy and trust Him more.
Him I all con-fide, For al-ways when I need Him, He's at my side.
yond life's troub-led sea, There I be-hold a ha-ven pre-pared for me.

CHORUS

I've an-chored in Je-sus, The storms of life I'll brave, I've an-chored in

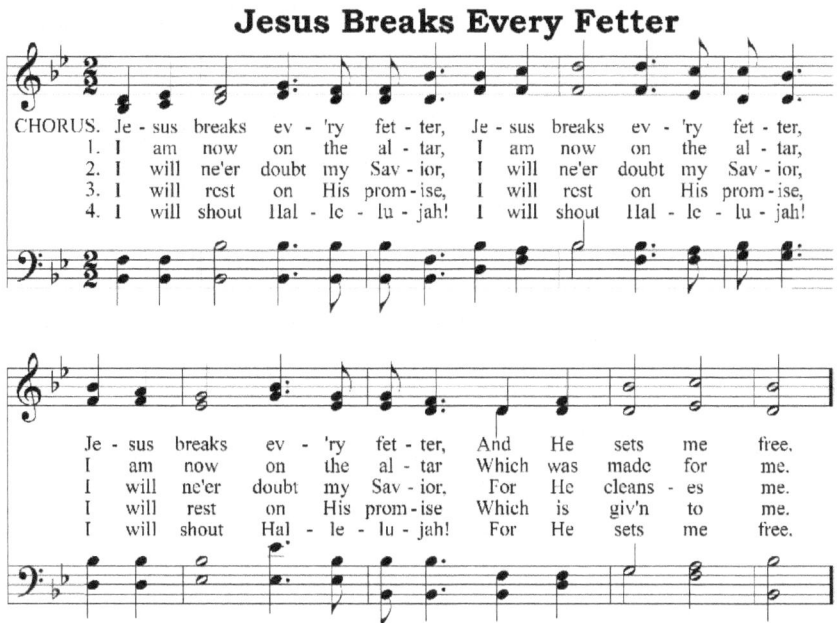

Words and Music: Anonymous

The Beautiful Garden of Prayer

60

1. There's a garden where Jesus is waiting, There's a place that is wondrously fair; For it glows with the light of His presence, 'Tis the beautiful garden of prayer.

2. There's a garden where Jesus is waiting, And I go with my burden and care, Just to learn from His lips words of comfort In the beautiful garden of prayer.

3. There's a garden where Jesus is waiting, And He bids you to come meet Him there; Just to bow, and receive a new blessing, In the beautiful garden of prayer.

CHORUS

O the beautiful garden, the garden of prayer, O the beautiful garden of prayer; There my Savior awaits, and He opens the gates To the beautiful garden of prayer.

Words and Music: Robert Lowry, 1874

I Am Going On With Jesus

I Surrender All

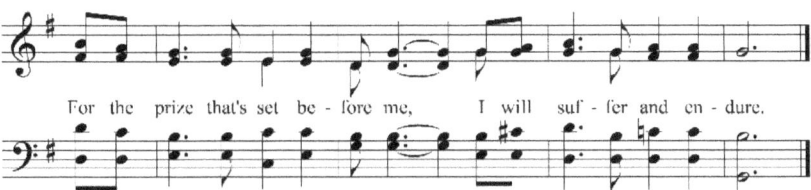

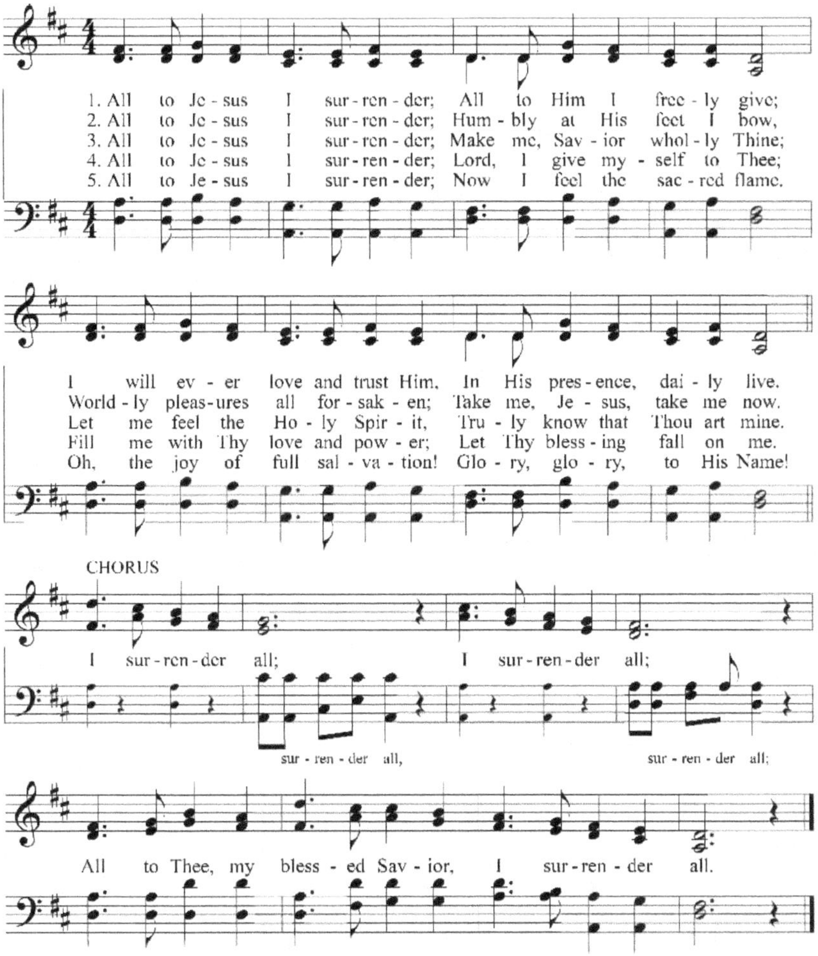

Words: Winfield S. Weeden, 1896
Music: Judson W. Van DeVenter

Softly and Tenderly

Words and Music: Will L. Thompson, 1880

Words and Music: Charles A. Tindley, 1905

Words: Ernest W. Blandy, 1890

Oh, How I Love Jesus

1. There is a Name I love to hear; I love to sing its worth;
It sounds like music in my ear, The sweetest Name on earth.
2. It tells me of a Savior's love, Who died to set me free;
It tells me of His precious blood, The sinner's perfect plea.
3. It tells of One whose loving heart Can feel my deepest woe;
Who in each sorrow bears a part That none can bear below.
4. This Name shall shed its fragrance still A-long this thorny road,
Shall sweetly smooth the rugged hill That leads me up to God.
5. And there with all the blood-bought throng, From sin and sorrow free,
I'll sing the new eternal song Of Jesus' love for me.

Oh, how I love Jesus, Oh, how I love Jesus, Oh, how I love Jesus, Because He first loved me!

Words: Frederick Whitfield, 1855

Is Your All on the Altar

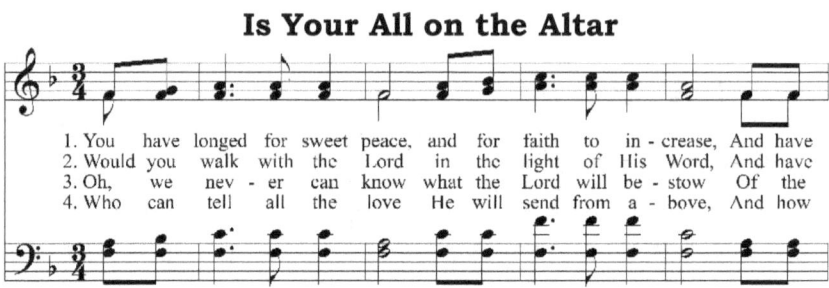

1. You have longed for sweet peace, and for faith to in-crease, And have
2. Would you walk with the Lord in the light of His Word, And have
3. Oh, we nev-er can know what the Lord will be-stow, Of the
4. Who can tell all the love He will send from a-bove, And how

ear - nest - ly, fer - vent - ly prayed; But you
peace and con - tent - ment al - way; You must
bless - ings for which we have prayed, Till our
hap - py our hearts will be made, Of the

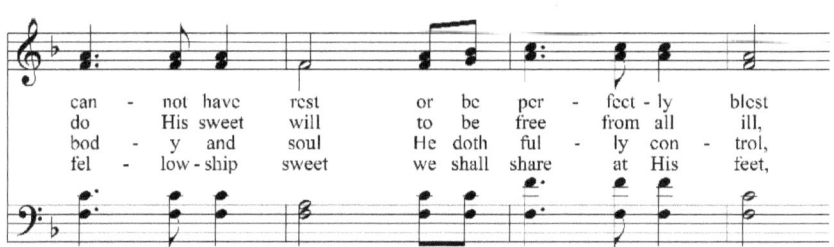

can - not have rest or be per - fect - ly blest
do His sweet will to be free from all ill,
bod - y and soul He doth ful - ly con - trol,
fel - low-ship sweet we shall share at His feet,

Un - til all on the al - tar is laid.
On the al - tar your all you must lay.
And our all on the al - tar is laid.
When our all on the al - tar is laid.

Words and Music: Elisha A. Hoffman, 1839 - 1929

Whiter Than Snow

1. Lord Jesus, I long to be perfectly whole;
   I want Thee forever to live in my soul,
   Break down ev'ry idol, cast out ev'ry foe;

2. Lord Jesus, look down from Thy throne in the skies,
   And help me to make a complete sacrifice;
   I give up myself, and whatever I know,

3. Lord Jesus, for this I most humbly entreat,
   I wait, blessed Lord, at Thy crucified feet;
   By faith, for my cleansing, I see Thy blood flow,

4. Lord Jesus, Thou seest I patiently wait,
   Come now, and within me a new heart create;
   To those who have sought Thee, Thou never saidst "No,"

CHORUS
Now wash me, and I shall be whiter than snow. Whiter than snow, yes, whiter than snow; Now wash me, and I shall be whiter than snow.

Words: James Nicholson, 1828-1876

Draw Me Nearer

1. I am Thine, O Lord, I have heard Thy voice, And it told Thy love to me; But I long to rise in the arms of faith And be clos-er drawn to Thee.
2. Con-se-crate me now to Thy ser-vice, Lord, By the pow'r of grace di-vine; Let my soul look up with a stead-fast hope, And my will be lost in Thine.
3. Oh, the pure de-light of a sin-gle hour That be-fore Thy throne I spend, When I kneel in prayer, and with Thee, my God I com-mune as friend with friend!
4. There are depths of love that I can-not know Till I cross the nar-row seas; There are heights of joy that I may not reach Till I rest in peace with Thee.

CHORUS

Draw me near-er, near-er bless-ed Lord, To the cross where Thou hast died; Draw me near-er, near-er, near-er bless-ed Lord, To Thy prec-ious bleed-ing side.

Words: Fannie J. Crosby, 1875

His Way with Thee

Words and Music: Cyrus S. Nusbaum, 1861 - 1937

I Need Jesus

1. I need Jesus, my need I now confess; No
2. I need Jesus, I need a friend like Him, A
3. I need Jesus, I need Him to the end; No

friend like Him in times of deep distress;
friend to guide when paths of life are dim;
one like Him, He is the sinner's Friend;

I need Jesus, the need I gladly own; Tho'
I need Jesus, when foes my soul assail; A-
I need Jesus, no other friend will do; So

some may bear their load alone, Yet I need Jesus.
lone I know I can but fail, So I need Jesus.
constant, kind, so strong and true, Yes, I need Jesus.

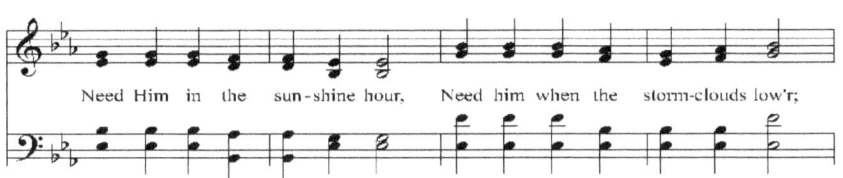

Words: George O. Webster
Music: Charles H. Gabriel

Fill Me Now

1. Hov-er o'er me, Ho-ly Spir-it, Bathe my trem-bling heart and brow;
2. Thou canst fill me, gra-cious Spir-it, Though I can-not tell Thee how;
3. I am weak-ness, full of weak-ness, At Thy sa-cred feet I bow;
4. Cleanse and com-fort, bless and save me, Bathe, O bathe my heart and brow;

Fill me with Thy hal-lowed pres-ence, Come, O come and fill me now.
But I need Thee, great-ly need Thee, Come, O come and fill me now.
Blest, di-vine, e-ter-nal Spir-it, Fill with pow'r, and fill me now.
Thou art com-fort-ing and sav-ing, Thou art sweet-ly fill-ing now.

CHORUS

Fill me now, fill me now, Je-sus, come and fill me now;

Fill me with Thy hal-lowed pres-ence, Come, O come and fill me now.

Words: Elwood H. Stokes, 1879

Face to Face

1. Face to face with Christ my Savior, Face to face how can it be;
When with rapture I behold Him, Jesus Christ who died for me?

2. Only faintly now I see Him, With the darkling veil between;
But a blessed day is coming, When His glory shall be seen.

3. What rejoicing in His presence, When are banished grief and pain!
When the crooked ways are straightened, And the dark things shall be plain!

4. Face to face— O blissful moment! Face to face to see and know;
Face to face with my Redeemer, Jesus Christ, who loves me so.

CHORUS
Face to face shall I behold Him, Far beyond the starry sky;
Face to face in all His glory, I shall see Him by and by!

Words: Grant C. Tullar, 1899

I'll Live On and On

1. 'Tis a sweet and glorious thought that comes to me, I'll live on, yes, I'll live on; Jesus saved my soul from death and now I'm free,
2. When my body's lying in the cold, cold clay, and on, yes, I'll live on; I will meet my Jesus in the judgment day,
3. In the glory-land, with God upon the throne, yes, I'll live on; Thru eternal ages singing, home, sweet home.

CHORUS
I'll live on, yes, I'll live on. I'll live on, yes, I'll live on, Thru eternity I'll live on, I'll live on, yes, I'll live on, Thru eternity I'll live on.

Words and Music: Thomas J. Laney, 1914

I Love to Tell the Story

Words: A. Katherine Hankey, 1866

84

At the Cross

1. Alas! and did my Savior bleed And did my Sov'reign die? Would He devote that sacred head For such a worm as I?
2. Thy body slain, sweet Jesus, Thine, And bathed in its own blood, While the firm mark of wrath divine, His soul in anguish stood.
3. Was it for crimes that I had done He groaned upon the tree? Amazing pity! grace unknown! And love beyond degree!
4. Well might the sun in darkness hide And shut his glories in, When Christ, the mighty Maker died, For man the creature's sin.
5. Thus might I hide my blushing face While His dear cross appears, Dissolve my heart in thankfulness, And melt my eyes to tears.
6. But drops of grief can ne'er repay The debt of love I owe; Here, Lord, I give myself away, 'Tis all that I can do.

CHORUS
At the cross, at the cross where I first saw the light, And the burden of my heart rolled away, (rolled away,) It was there by faith I received my sight, And now I am happy all the day!

Words and Music: Isaac Watts, 1775

Look and Live

1. I've a message from the Lord, Hallelujah! The message unto you I'll give. 'Tis recorded in His Word, Hallelujah! It is only that you "look and live."
2. I've a message full of love, Hallelujah! A message, O my friend, for you. 'Tis a message from above, Hallelujah! Jesus said it, and I know 'tis true.
3. Life is offered unto you. Hallelujah! Eternal life your soul shall have If you'll only look to Him. Hallelujah! Look to Jesus, who alone can save.
4. I will tell you how I came, Hallelujah! To Jesus when He made me whole: 'Twas believing on His name, Hallelujah! I trusted and He saved my soul.

CHORUS
"Look and live," my brother, live. Look to Jesus now and live. 'Tis recorded in His Word, Hallelujah! It is only that you "look and live."

Words and Music: William A. Ogden, 1887

Seeking For Me

1. Jesus, my Savior, to Bethlehem came, Laid in a manger to sorrow and shame; Oh, it was wonderful, blest be His Name, Seeking for me, for me,
2. Jesus, my Savior, in mercy and love, Came from the mansions of Heaven above, Tenderly pleading with sinners like me, Pleading for me, for me,
3. Jesus, my Savior, the same as of old, While I did wander afar from the fold, Gently and long He hath pled with my soul, Calling for me, for me,
4. Jesus, my Savior, will come from on high, Sweet is the promise as weary years fly; Oh, I shall see Him descending the sky, Coming for me, for me,

CHORUS
Seeking for me, seeking for me, Seeking for me, seeking for me, Oh, it was wonderful, blest be His Name, Seeking for me, for me.
Pleading for me, pleading for me, Pleading for me, pleading for me, Tenderly pleading for sinners like me, Pleading for me, for me.
Calling for me, calling for me, Calling for me, calling for me, Gently and long He hath pled with my soul, Calling for me, for me.
Coming for me, coming for me, Coming for me, coming for me, Oh, I shall see Him descending the sky, Coming for me, for me.

Words and Music: E. E. Hasty, 1895

Sow Righteous Seed

1. There is com-ing a day, When to judg-ment we must go. To reap as in life you have sown. Death e-
2. If you win life e-ternal, There is no time to lose. Look a-round you, the fields are white. Go ye
3. Ev-'ry day pass-ing by, We are sow-ing the seed. Fruits of life or death you have sown. If you
4. Ev-'ry act you per-form Is a seed to some-one. And the in-flu-ence will nev-er die. Just be

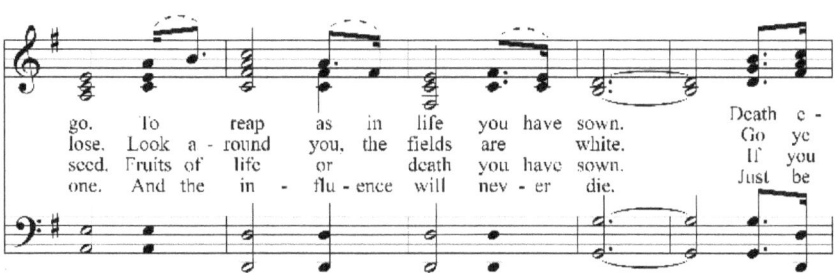

ter-nal we will reap. If we sow to the flesh, Heav-en's joy will not be known.
forth to the field. Sow and reap gold-en grain, Soon will fall the dark shad-ows of night.
reap what you sow. To that land you will go, To that bright hap-py home o-ver there.
care-ful each day. What you do and what you say. You will reap it a-gain some-day.

Words: A. A. Childs

90

Higher Ground

1. I'm press-ing on the up-ward way, New heights I'm gain-ing ev-'ry day;
2. My heart has no de-sire to stay Where doubts a-rise and fears dis-may;
3. I want to live a-bove the world, Tho' Sa-tan's darts at me are hurled;
4. I want to scale the ut-most height And catch a gleam of glo-ry bright;

Still pray-ing as I on-ward, bound, "Lord plant my feet on high-er ground."
Tho' some may dwell where these a-bound, My prayer, my aim is high-er ground.
For faith has caught the joy-ful sound, The song of saints on high-er ground.
But still I'll pray till Heav'n I've found, "Lord, lead me on to high-er ground.

CHORUS

Lord, lift me up and let me stand, By faith, on Heav-en's ta-ble-land,
A high-er plane than I have found; Lord, plant my feet on high-er ground.

Words: Johnson Oatman, Jr., 1898

My Faith Looks Up to Thee

Words: Ray Palmer, 1830

Words and Music: Ruth C. Jones, 1902

94

His Yoke Is Easy

1. The Lord is my shepherd; I shall not want. He mak-eth me down to lie__ In pas-tures green He lead-eth me The qui-et wa-ters by.
2. My soul cri-eth out: "Re-store me a-gain, And give me the strength to take The nar-row path of right-cous-ness, E'en for His own name's sake."
3. Yea, tho' I should walk the val-ley of death, Yet why should I fear from ill?__ For Thou art with me, and Thy rod And staff me com-fort still.__

CHORUS
His yoke is ea-sy; His bur-den is light. I've found it so; I've found it so. He lead-eth me by day and by night Where liv-ing wa-ters flow.

Words and Music: Ralph E. Hudson, 1885

Words: Anonymous

The Last Mile of the Way

1. If I walk in the path-way of du-ty, If I
2. If for Christ I pro-claim the glad sto-ry, If I
3. Here the dear-est of ties we must sev-er, Tears of
4. And if here I have earn-est-ly striv-en, And have

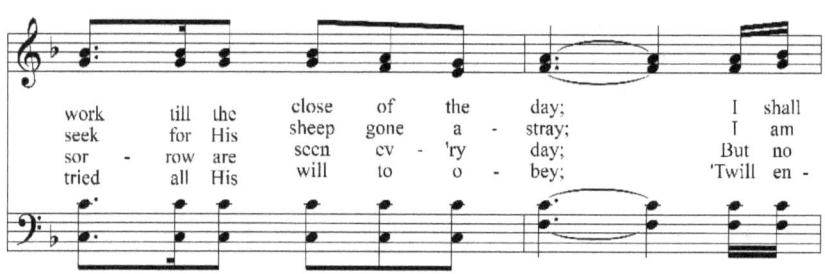

work till the close of the day; I shall
seek for His sheep gone a-stray; I am
sor-row are seen ev-'ry day; But no
tried all His will to o-bey; 'Twill en-

see the great King in His beau-ty
sure He will show me His glo-ry
sick-ness, no sigh-ing for-ev-er
hance all the rap-ture of heav-en

When I've gone the last mile of the way.

97

Words: William E. Marks, 1936
Music: Johnson Oatman, Jr.

98

Mountain Railroad

1. Life is like a moun-tain rail-way, With an en-gin-eer that's brave;
2. You will roll up grades of tri-al; You will cross the bridge of strife;
3. You will of-ten find ob-struc-tions, Look for storms and wind and rain;
4. As you roll a-cross the tres-tle, Span-ning Jor-dan's swell-ing tide,

We must make the run suc-cess-ful, From the cra-dle to the grave;
See that Christ is your con-duc-tor On this light-ning train of life;
On a fill, or curve, or tres-tle They will al-most ditch your train;
You be-hold the Un-ion De-pot In-to which your train will glide;

Watch the curves, the fills, the tun-nels; Nev-er fal-ter, nev-er fail;
Al-ways mind-ful of ob-struc-tion, Do your du-ty nev-er fail;
Put your trust a-lone in Je-sus, Nev-er fal-ter, nev-er fail;
There you'll meet the Su-p'rin-ten-dent, God, the Fath-er, God the Son,

Keep your hands up-on the throt-tle, And your eyes up-on the rail.
Keep your hands up-on the throt-tle, And your eyes up-on the rail.
Keep your hands up-on the throt-tle, And your eyes up-on the rail.
With the heart-y, joy-ous plau-dit, "Wea-ry Pil-grim, wel-come home."

Bless-ed Sav-ior, Thou wilt guide us, Till we reach that bliss-ful shore,

Where the an-gels wait to join us In Thy praise for-ev-er-more.

Words: Eliza R. Snow; ref. attr. to M. E. Abbey

Beulah Land

1. I've reached the land of corn and wine, And all its riches freely mine;
   Here shines undimmed one blissful day, For all my night has passed away.
2. My Savior comes and walks with me, And sweet communion here have we;
   He gently leads me by His hand, For this is Heaven's borderland.
3. A sweet perfume upon the breeze Is borne from ever vernal trees,
   And flow'rs, that never fading grow, Where streams of life forever flow.
4. The zephyrs seem to float to me, Sweet sound of Heaven's melody,
   As angels with the white-robed throng Join in the sweet Redemption song.

CHORUS

O Beulah Land, sweet Beulah Land, As on thy highest mount I stand,
I look away across the sea, Where mansions are prepared for me,
And view the shining glory-shore, My Heav'n, my home forevermore.

Words: Edgar P. Stites, 1876

All Hail the Power of Jesus' Name

1. All hail the pow'r of Jesus' name!
2. Ye chos - en seed of Is - rael's race,
3. Let ev - 'ry kin - dred, ev - 'ry tribe
4. O that with yon - der sa - cred throng

Let an - gels pro - strate fall, Let an - gels pro - strate fall:
Ye ran - somed from the fall, Ye ran - somed from the fall,
On this ter - res - trial ball, On this ter - res - trial ball,
We at His feet may fall, We at His fee may fall!

Bring forth the roy - al di - a - dem,
Hail Him who saves you by His grace,
To Him all maj - es - ty as - cribe,
We'll join the ev - er - last - ing song,

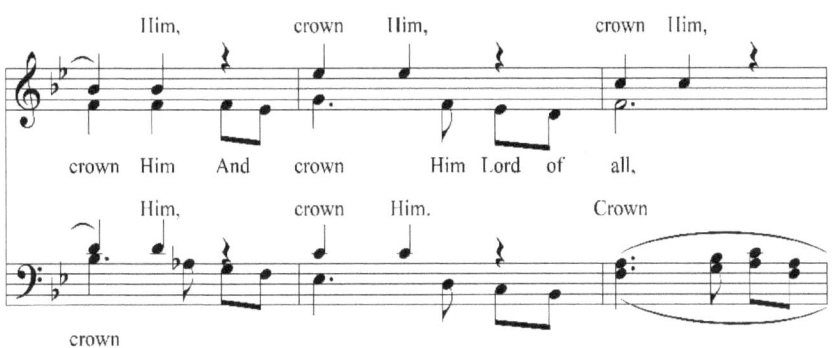

Words: Edward Perronet, 1726 – 1792
Music: James Ellor, 1838

A New Name in Glory

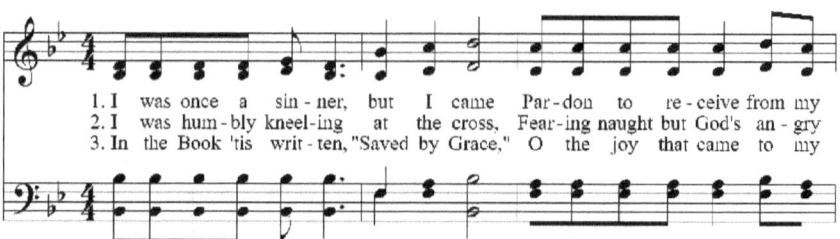

1. I was once a sin-ner, but I came Par-don to re-ceive from my
2. I was hum-bly kneel-ing at the cross, Fear-ing naught but God's an-gry
3. In the Book 'tis writ-ten, "Saved by Grace," O the joy that came to my

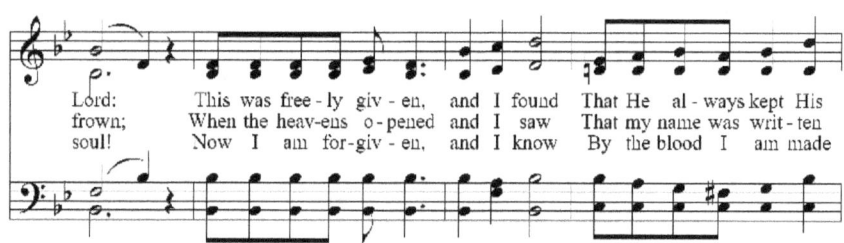

Lord; This was free-ly giv-en, and I found That He al-ways kept His
frown; When the heav-ens o-pened and I saw That my name was writ-ten
soul! Now I am for-giv-en, and I know By the blood I am made

word (kept His word). There's a new name writ-ten down in glo-ry,
down (writ-ten down).
whole (am made whole).

And it's mine, O yes, it's mine! And the
(And it's mine, Yes it's mine!)

103

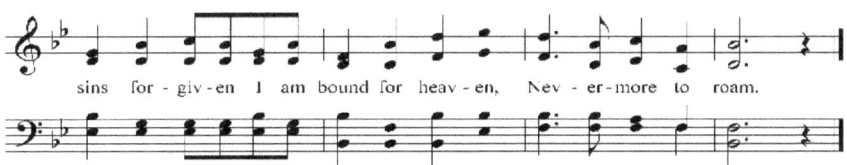

Words and Music: C. Austin Miles, 1910 © 1987 Southern Faith Songs

104

Where Jesus Is, 'Tis Heaven

1. Since Christ my soul from sin set free, This world has been a Heav'n to me;
2. Once Heav-en seemed a far-off place, Till Je-sus showed His smil-ing face;
3. What mat-ters where on earth we dwell? On moun-tain top, or in the dell,

And 'mid earth's sor-rows and its woe, 'Tis Heav'n my Je-sus here to know.
Now it's be-gun with-in my soul, 'Twill last while end-less ag-es roll.
In cot-tage, or a man-sion fair, Where Je-sus is, 'tis Heav-en there.

CHORUS

Oh, hal-le-lu-jah, yes 'tis Heav'n, 'Tis Heav'n to know my sins for-giv'n;
On land or sea, what mat-ters where? Where Je-sus is, 'tis Heav-en there.

Words: Charles J. Butler, 1898

Oh, I Want to See Him

1. As I journey through the land, singing as I go,
Pointing souls to Calvary— to the crimson flow,
Many arrows pierce my soul from without, within;
But my Lord leads me on, through Him I must win.

2. When in service for my Lord dark may be the night,
But I'll cling more close to Him, He will give me light;
Satan's snares may vex my soul, turn my thoughts aside;
But my Lord goes ahead, leads what-e'er betide.

3. When in valleys low I look toward the mountain height,
And behold my Savior there, leading in the fight,
With a tender hand outstretched toward the valley low,
Guiding me, I can see, as I onward go.

4. When before me billows rise from the mighty deep,
Then my Lord directs my bark; He doth safely keep.
And He leads me gently on through this world below;
He's a real Friend to me, oh I love Him so.

Words and Music: Rufus H. Cornelius, 1916

We're Marching to Zion

1. Come, we that love the Lord, And let our joys be known; Join in a song with sweet ac-cord, Join in a song with sweet ac-cord, And thus sur-round the throne, And thus sur-round the throne.
2. The sor-rows of the mind Be ban-ished from the place; Re-li-gion nev-er was de-signed, Re-li-gion nev-er was de-signed To make our pleas-ures less, To make our pleas-ures less.
3. Let those re-fuse to sing, Who nev-er knew our God;— But child-ren of the heav'n-ly King, But child-ren of the heav'n-ly King May speak their joys a-broad, May speak their joys a-broad.
4. The men of grace have found Glo-ry be-gan be-low;— Ce-les-tial fruits on earth-ly ground, Ce-les-tial fruits on earth-ly ground From faith and hope may grow, From faith and hope may grow.
5. The hill of Zi-on yields A thou-sand sa-cred sweets Be-fore we reach the heav'n-ly fields, Be-fore we reach the heav'n-ly fields, Or walk the gold-en streets, Or walk the gold-en streets.
6. Then let our songs a-broad, And ev-'ry tear be dry;— We're march-ing thro' Im-man-uel's ground, We're march-ing thro' Im-man-uel's ground To fair-er worlds on high, To fair-er worlds on high.

CHORUS
We're march-ing to Zi-on, Beau-ti-ful, beau-ti-ful Zi-on We're march-ing up-ward to Zi-on, The beau-ti-ful cit-y of God.

Words: Isaac Watts, 1707

Words and Music: C. Austin Miles, 1911

112

When We All Get to Heaven

1. Sing the wond-rous love of Je-sus, Sing His mer-cy and His grace;
2. While we walk the pil-grim path-way, Clouds will o-ver-spread the sky;
3. Let us then be true and faith-ful, Trust-ing, serv-ing, ev-'ry day.
4. On-ward to the prize be-fore us! Soon His beau-ty we'll be-hold;

In the man-sions bright and bless-ed He'll pre-pare for us a place.
But when trav-'ling days are o-ver, Not a shad-ow, not a sigh.
Just one glimpse of Him in glo-ry Will the toils of life re-pay.
Soon the pear-ly gates will o-pen; We shall tread the streets of gold.

CHORUS

When we all get to heav-en, What a day of re-joic-ing that will be! When we all see Je-sus, We'll sing and shout the vic-to-ry!

Words: Eliza E. Hewitt, 1898

Won't It Be Wonderful There

1. When with the Sav-ior we en-ter the glo-ry-land, Won't it be won-der-ful there? End-ed the trou-bles and cares of the sto-ry-land,
2. Walk-ing and talk-ing with Christ, the su-per-nal One, Won't it be won-der-ful there? Prais-ing, a-dor-ing the match-less e-ter-nal One,
3. There where the tem-pest will nev-er be sweep-ing us, Won't it be won-der-ful there? Sure that for-ev-er the Lord will be keep-ing us,

Won't it be won-der-ful there?

CHORUS

Won't it be won-der-ful there, hav-ing no bur-dens to bear? Joy-ous-ly sing-ing with heart-bells all ring-ing, O won't it be won-der-ful there?

Words: James Rowe, 1930

114

Just Over In Glory Land

115

Words: James W. Acuff, 1906

When the Roll Is Called Up Yonder

116

Words and Music: James M. Black, 1893

118

One Day

Words: Charles H. Marsh
Music: J. Wilbur Chapman

120

Hold to God's Unchanging Hand

1. Time is filled with swift tran-si-tion, Naught of earth un-moved can stand,
2. Trust in Him who will not leave you, What-so-ev-er years may bring,
3. Cov-et not this world's vain rich-es That so rap-id-ly de-cay;
4. When your jour-ney is com-plet-ed, If to God you have been true;

Build your hopes on things e-ter-nal, Hold to God's un-chang-ing hand.
If by earth-ly friends for-sak-en Still more close-ly to Him cling;
Seek to gain the heav'n-ly treas-ures, They will nev-er pass a-way.
Fair and bright the home in glo-ry Your en-rap-tured soul will view.

CHORUS

Hold to God's un-chang-ing hand, Hold to God's un-chang-ing hand;
to His hand, to His hand.

Build your hopes on things e-ter-nal, Hold to God's un-chang-ing hand.

Words: Jennie Wilson, 1860 - 1909

On Jordan's Stormy Banks

Words and Music: Samuel Stennett, 1787

Words and Music: Frank C. Huston, 1909

I Will Praise Him

1. When I saw the cleans-ing foun-tain
2. Tho' the way seems straight and nar-row,
3. Then God's fire up-on the al-tar
4. Bless-ed be the name of Je-sus!
5. Glo-ry, glo-ry to the Fath-er!

O-pen wide for all my sin,
All I claimed was swept a-way;
Of my heart was set a-flame;
I'm so glad He took me in;
Glo-ry, glo-ry to the Son!

I o-beyed the Spir-it's woo-ing,
My am-bi-tions, plans, and wish-es,
I shall nev-er cease to praise Him,
He's for-giv-en my trans-gres-sions,
Glo-ry, glo-ry to the Spir-it!

When He said, "Wilt thou be clean?"
At my feet in ash-es lay.
Glo-ry, glo-ry to His name!
He has cleansed my heart from sin.
Glo-ry to the Three in One!

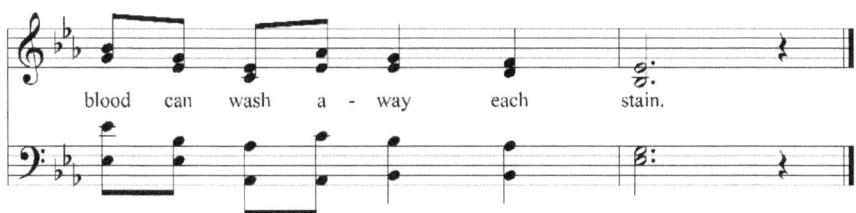

Words and Music: Margaret J. Harris, 1898

I'd Rather Have Jesus

127
CHORUS

Than to be the king of a vast domain

And be held in sin's dread sway;

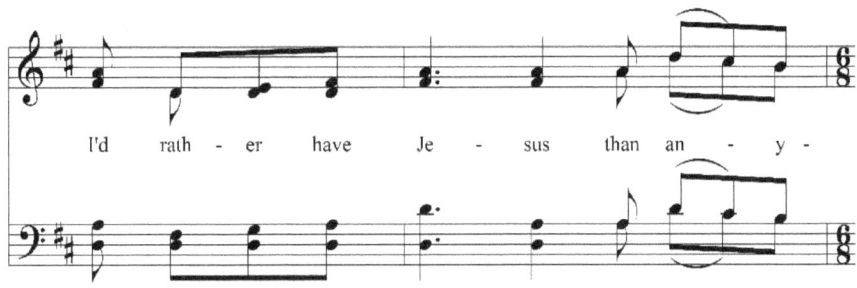
I'd rather have Jesus than any-

thing This world affords to day.

Words and Music: Rhea F. Miller, 1922

It Took a Miracle

1. My Father is omnipotent, And that you can't deny;
A God of might and miracles, 'Tis written in the sky.
2. Thou here His glory has been shown, We still can't fully see
The wonders of His might, His throne; 'Twill take eternity.
3. The Bible tells us of His pow'r And wisdom all way thru,
And ev'ry little bird and flow'r Are testimonies too.

CHORUS
It took a miracle to put the stars in place, It took a miracle to hang the world in space; But when He saved my soul, Cleansed and made me whole, It took a miracle of love and grace!

Words and Music: John W. Peterson

Words: Priscilla J. Owens, 1829-1907

131

Words: Charles H. Gabriel
Music: W. C. Martin

My Jesus, I Love Thee

1. My Jesus, I love Thee, I know Thou art mine. For
2. I love Thee, because Thou hast first loved me, And
3. I'll love Thee in life, I will love Thee in death, And
4. In mansions of glory and endless delight, I'll

Thee all the follies of sin I resign; My
purchased my pardon on Calvary's tree; I
praise Thee as long as Thou lendest me breath; And
ever adore Thee in heaven so bright; I'll

gracious Redeemer, my Savior art Thou; If
love Thee for wearing the thorns on Thy brow; If
say when the death-dew lies cold on my brow; If
sing with the glittering crown on my brow; If

ever I loved Thee, my Jesus, 'tis now.
ever I loved Thee, my Jesus, 'tis now.
ever I loved Thee, my Jesus, 'tis now.
ever I loved Thee, my Jesus, 'tis now.

Words: William R. Featherston, 1864

Pass Me Not, O Gentle Savior

1. Pass me not, O gentle Savior, Hear my humble cry;
2. Let me at a throne of mercy Find a sweet relief;
3. Trusting only in Thy merit, Would I seek Thy face;
4. Thou the spring of all my comfort, More than life to me,

While on others Thou art calling, Do not pass me by.
Kneeling there in deep contrition, Help my unbelief.
Heal my wounded, broken spirit, Save me by Thy grace.
Whom have I on earth beside Thee, Whom in Heav'n but Thee.

CHORUS

Savior, Savior, Hear my humble cry,

While on others Thou are calling, Do not pass me by.

Words and Music: Fannie Crosby, 1868

The Name of Jesus

1. The name of Jesus is so sweet, I love its music to repeat; It makes my joys full and complete, The precious name of Jesus.
2. I love the name of Him whose heart Knows all my griefs and bears a part; Who bids all anxious fears depart— I love the precious name.
3. That name I fondly love to hear, It never fails my heart to cheer, Its music dries the falling tear; Exalt the precious name.
4. No word of man can ever tell How sweet the name I love so well; Oh, let its praises ever swell, Oh, praise the precious name.

CHORUS
"Jesus," oh, how sweet the name! "Jesus," ev'ry day the same; "Jesus," let all saints proclaim Its worthy praise forever.

Words: W. C. Martin, 1902

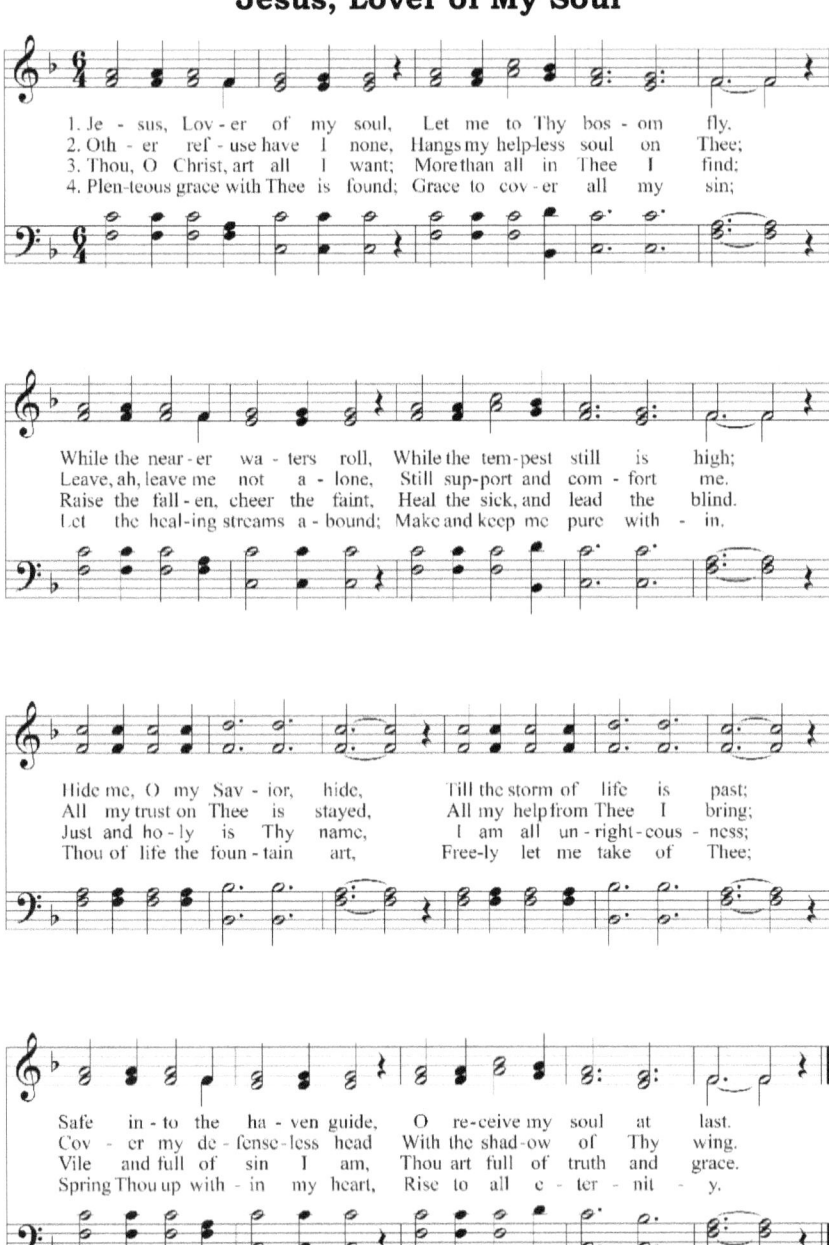

Jesus, Lover of My Soul

1. Jesus, Lover of my soul, Let me to Thy bosom fly, While the nearer waters roll, While the tempest still is high; Hide me, O my Savior, hide, Till the storm of life is past; Safe into the haven guide, O receive my soul at last.

2. Other refuge have I none, Hangs my helpless soul on Thee; Leave, ah, leave me not alone, Still support and comfort me. All my trust on Thee is stayed, All my help from Thee I bring; Cover my defenseless head With the shadow of Thy wing.

3. Thou, O Christ, art all I want; More than all in Thee I find; Raise the fallen, cheer the faint, Heal the sick, and lead the blind. Just and holy is Thy name, I am all unrighteousness; Vile and full of sin I am, Thou art full of truth and grace.

4. Plenteous grace with Thee is found; Grace to cover all my sin; Let the healing streams abound; Make and keep me pure within. Thou of life the fountain art, Freely let me take of Thee; Spring Thou up within my heart, Rise to all eternity.

Words: Charles Wesley

138

Trust And Obey

1. When we walk with the Lord In the Light of His Word What a glory He sheds on our way! While we do His good will, He abides with us still, And with all who will trust and obey.
2. Not a shad-ow can rise, Not a cloud in the skies, But His smile quick-ly drives it a-way! Not a doubt or a fear, Not a sigh nor a tear, Can a-bide while we trust and obey.
3. Not a bur-den we bear, Not a sor-row we share, But our toil He doth rich-ly re-pay! Not a grief nor a loss, Not a frown or a cross, But is blest if we trust and obey.
4. But we nev-er can prove, The de-lights of His love Un-til all on the al-tar we lay; For the fav-or He shows, And the joy He be-stows, Are for them who will trust and obey.
5. Then in fel-low-ship sweet We will sit at His feet, Or we'll walk by His side in the way; What He says we will do, Where He sends we will go, Nev-er fear, on-ly trust and obey.

CHORUS
Trust and obey, for there's no oth-er way To be happy in Jesus, But to trust and obey.

Words: John H. Sammis, 1846 - 1919

Trusting Jesus

1. Sim-ply trust-ing ev-'ry day, Trust-ing through a storm-y way;
2. Bright-ly doth His Spir-it shine In-to this poor heart of mine;
3. Sing-ing if my way is clear; Pray-ing if the path be drear;
4. Trust-ing Him while life shall last, Trust-ing Him till earth be past;

E-ven when my faith is small, Trust-ing Je-sus, that is all.
While He leads I can-not fall; Trust-ing Je-sus, that is all.
If in dan-ger, for Him call; Trust-ing Je-sus, that is all.
Till with-in the jas-per wall: Trust-ing Je-sus, that is all.

CHORUS
Trust-ing as the mo-ments fly, Trust-ing as the days go by;
Trust-ing Him what-e'er be-fall, Trust-ing Je-sus, that is all.

Words: Edgar P. Stites, 1876

Leaving All to Follow Jesus

Words: Ida M. Budd, 1898

Words: Johnson Oatman, Jr., 1897

142

Praise Thy Name

1. Bless-ed Jesus, Thou hast saved me, Thou hast filled my heart with joy; In Thy name I have salvation, Through Thy precious cleansing blood.
2. Thou art God, my Holy Father, Bread of life thou art to me; Living water from the fountain, Thou hast giv'n me liberty.
3. Thou hast borne my sins and sickness, Thou from death hast set me free. Thou hast gone and prepared a mansion Where I may dwell eternally.
4. I have called Thee, "Abba Father." I have stayed my heart on Thee, Son of God, Thou Holy Spirit, Thou art all in all to me.

CHORUS
Praise Thy name, praise Thy name, Thou Rock of my salvation, Hallelujah! Praise Thy name.

Words and Music: R. C. Lawson, 1920

Glory to His Name

1. Down at the cross where my Savior died, Down where for cleansing from sin I cried, There to my heart was the blood applied; Glory to His Name!
2. I am so wondrously saved from sin, Jesus so sweetly abides within, There at the cross where He took me in; Glory to His Name!
3. Oh, precious fountain that saves from sin, I am so glad I have entered in; There Jesus saves me and keeps me clean; Glory to His Name!
4. Come to this fountain so rich and sweet, Cast thy poor soul at the Savior's feet; Plunge in today, and be made complete; Glory to His Name!

CHORUS
Glory to His Name, Glory to His Name; There to my heart was the blood applied; Glory to His Name!

Words: Elisha A. Hoffman, 1839 - 1929

144

God Is Great In My Soul

1. God's greatness is seen, In the Heav'n above, In the world He established on the floods, The glory of His greatness Seen on Calvary, Where He shed His precious Blood.

CHORUS
God is great, greatly to be praised, God is great in my soul. God is great in my soul.

2. When Jesus He died, the veil was rent in twain, That separated man from God, But now, by faith, we have access to Him, All thru His precious blood.

Words and Music: R. C. Lawson

Come, Thou Almighty King

1. Come, Thou Almighty King, Help us Thy name to sing, Help us to praise: Father, all glorious, O'er all victorious, Come, and reign over us, Ancient of Days.
2. Come, Thou Incarnate Word, Gird on Thy mighty sword, Our prayer attend: Come, and Thy people bless, And give Thy word success; Spirit of holiness, On us descend.
3. Come, Holy Comforter, Thy sacred witness bear In this glad hour: Thou who almighty art, Now rule in ev'ry heart, And ne'er from us depart, Spirit of pow'r.
4. To the great One in Three Eternal praises be, Hence evermore. His sovereign majesty May we in glory see, And to eternity Love and adore.

Words: Charles Wesley, 1757

To God Be the Glory

146

Tis So Sweet to Trust in Jesus

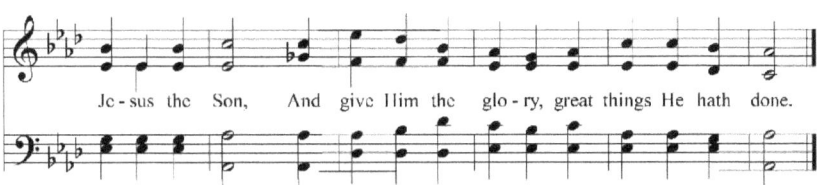

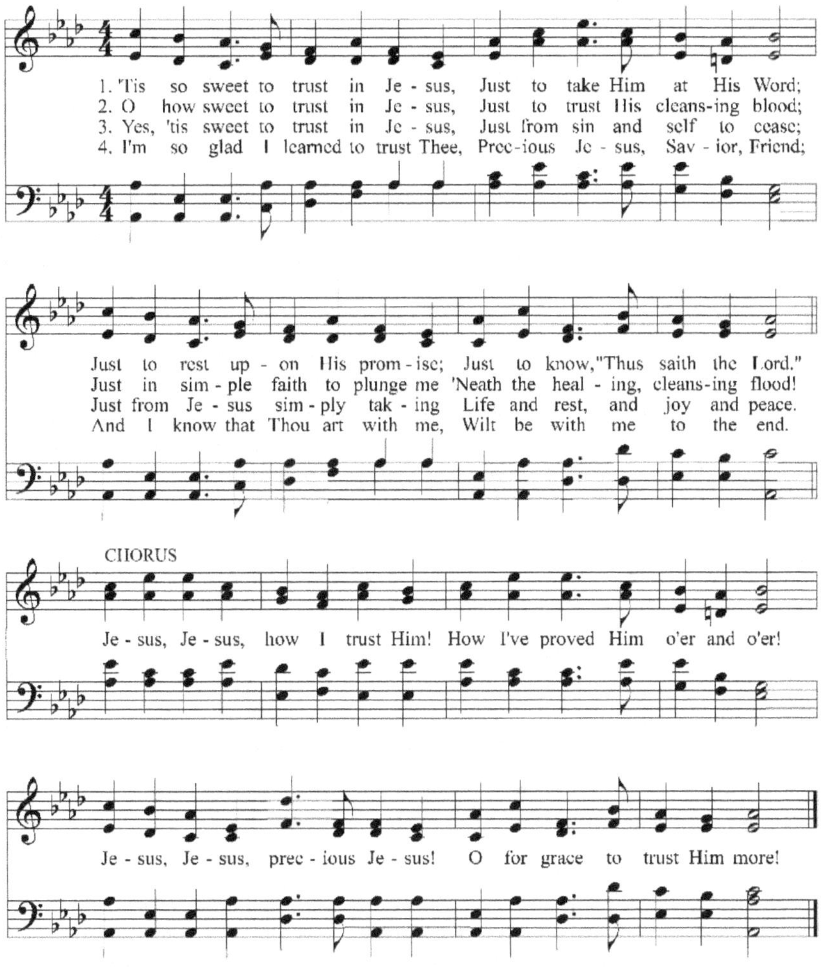

Words: Louisa M. R. Stead, 1882
Music: William J. Kirkpatrick, 1882

By the Rivers of Babylon

1. When the Lord turned a-gain the cap-tiv-i-ty of Zi-on, We were like them that dream, And our mouths were filled with laugh-ter, And our tongues with sing-ing. O give thanks un-to the Lord, For His mer-cy en-dur-eth for-ev-er. Be-fore God sent His Spir-it, We were all in sin; We could not sing His songs in a strange land, But thanks be un-to God we're

2. We have all been brought in to the full-ness of His Spir-it— In His name we have be-lieved, And His prom-ise we've re-ceived And with joy we'll serve Him. Hal-le-lu-jah to the Lamb For His mer-cy en-dur-eth for-ev-er. Come out of her my peo-ple Par-take not of her sin— Be filled with right-cous-ness if you would en-ter in, O glo-ry be to God we're

Words: R. C. Lawson, 1922
Music: Karl F. Smith

150

Holiness unto the Lord

1. "Called un-to ho-li-ness," Church of our God,
2. "Called un-to ho-li-ness," child-ren of light,
3. "Called un-to ho-li-ness," praise His dear name!
4. "Called un-to ho-li-ness," bride of the Lamb,

Pur-chase of Je-sus, re-deemed by His blood;
Walk-ing with Je-sus in gar-ments of white;
This bless-ed se-cret to faith now made plain;
Wait-ing the Bride-groom's re-turn-ing a-gain!

Called from the world and its i-dols to flee,
Rai-ment un-sull-ied, nor tar-nished with sin;
Not our own right-eous-ness, but Christ with-in,
Lift up your heads, for the day draw-eth near

Called from the bond-age of sin to be free.
God's Ho-ly Spir-it a-bid-ing with-in.
Liv-ing, and reign-ing, and sav-ing from sin.
When in His beau-ty the King shall ap-pear.

151

Words and Music: Lelia N. Morris, 1900

The Comforter Has Come

1. O spread the tidings 'round, wherever man is found, Wherever human hearts and human woes abound: Let ev'ry Christian tongue proclaim the joyful sound: The Comforter has come!

2. The long, long night is past, the morning breaks at last, And hushed the dreadful wail and fury of the blast, As o'er the golden hills the day advances fast! The Comforter has come!

3. Lo, the great King of kings, with healing in His wings, To ev'ry captive soul a full deliv-'rance brings; And thro' the vacant cells the song of triumph rings; The Comforter has come!

4. O boundless love divine! how shall this tongue of mine To wond'ring mortals tell the matchless grace divine That I, a child of hell, should in His image shine! The Comforter has come!

153

Words: Frank Bottome, 1890
Music: William J. Kirkpatrick, 1890

154

The Name of God

1. There's a secret God has hidden, Thru the ages was it sealed; Now to those who seek to know Him, Is the mystery revealed. Far back in the early ages, A-bram knew our precious Lord, And the
2. Moses learned "I Am" had sent Him, When he wished God's name to know, And by cloud and fire, Jehovah, Like a shepherd led them thru. Thus His dwelling place was with them, As they journeyed, and in camp; To their
3. When at last they crossed the Jordan, Captain of the Lord's host came, An-gel of the Lord was with them, Al-tho' no one knew His name. Then our Lord vanished in-to day. Then the temple, To His people closer came; And the
4. When the everlasting Father's Temple was a house of clay, Then the glory shone still brighter, Darkness spoken clear and plain; Christ in you, the glorious name of Jesus, As a day spring did appear, Which fore-
5. Manna true came down from heaven, Bearing with it Jesus' name, Held in mys-tery thro' the ages; Now 'tis the hope of glory, Lord of heaven, Lord of hosts; And in

156

The Great I Am

1. God is Elohim of all the holy prophets,
   The El-shaddai of all the seers and sages,
   He's the Mighty One of all the sacred pages.
2. He's Jehovah God, the coming King of glory,
   He's the true Nissi, the Lord of grace and favor,
   He is Jesus Christ, Redeemer, Friend and Savior.
3. He's the strong Rophi, the healing one of heaven,
   He's the Holy Ghost, the Spirit pour'd from glory,
   He's the sacred One of all the gospel story,

He's the great, He's the great I Am.

Words and Music: S. K. Grimes, 1924

157

158

All in Him

1. The mighty God is Jesus, The Prince of peace is He, The everlasting Father, The King eternally, The wonderful in wisdom By whom all things were made; The fullness of the Godhead in Jesus is displayed.

2. Emmanuel, God with us, Jehovah, Lord of hosts! The omnipresent Spirit, Who fills the universe, The Advocate, the High Priest, The Lamb for sinners slain. The Author of redemption; O glory to His name!

3. The Alpha and Omega, Beginning and the end, The Living Word incarnate, The helpless sinner's Friend, Our wisdom and perfection, Our righteousness and pow'r, Yea, all we need in Jesus We find this very hour.

4. "Our God for whom we've waited" Will be the glad refrain Of Israel re-created, When Jesus comes again; Lo! He will come and save us, Our King and Priest to be, For in Him dwells all fullness, And Lord of all is He.

159

Words and Music: George R. Farrow, 1920

God Leads Us Along

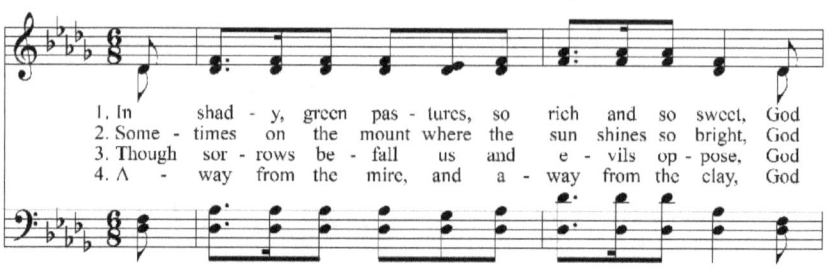

1. In shad-y, green pas-tures, so rich and so sweet, God
2. Some-times on the mount where the sun shines so bright, God
3. Though sor-rows be-fall us and e-vils op-pose, God
4. A-way from the mire, and a-way from the clay, God

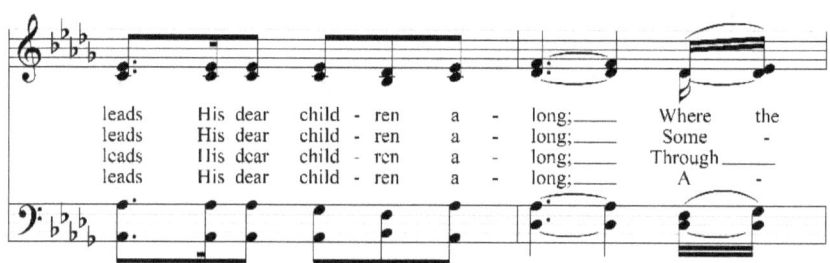

leads His dear child-ren a-long; Where the
leads His dear child-ren a-long; Some-
leads His dear child-ren a-long; Through
leads His dear child-ren a-long; A-

wat-er's cool flow bathes the wear-y one's feet, God
times in the val-ley, in dark-est of night, God
grace we can con-quer, de-feat all our foes, God
way up in glo-ry, e-ter-ni-ty's day, God

leads His dear child-ren a-long.
leads His dear child-ren a-long.
leads His dear child-ren a-long.
leads His dear child-ren a-long.

Words and Music: George A. Young, 1903

162

Yesterday, Today, Forever

Yes - ter - day, to - day, for - ev - er, Je - sus is the same.
All may change, but Je - sus nev - er! Glo - ry to His name!
Glo - ry to His name! Glo - ry to His name!
All may change, but Je - sus nev - er! Glo - ry to His name!

Yield Not to Temptation

1. Yield not to temp - ta - tion, for yield - ing is sin;
2. Shun e - vil con - pan - ions, bad lan - guage dis - dain,
3. To him that o'er - com - eth, God giv - eth a crown;

164

I've Believed the True Report

1. I've be-lieved the true re-port, Hal-le-lu-jah to the Lamb! I have
2. I'm a king and priest to God, Hal-le-lu-jah to the Lamb! By the
3. I have passed the out-er veil, Hal-le-lu-jah to the Lamb! Which did
4. I'm with-in the ho-liest pale, Hal-le-lu-jah to the Lamb! I have

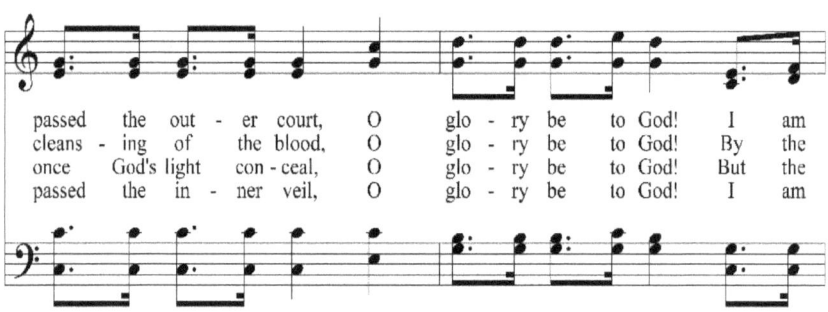

passed the out-er court, O glo-ry be to God! I am
cleans-ing of the blood, O glo-ry be to God! By the
once God's light con-ceal, O glo-ry be to God! But the
passed the in-ner veil, O glo-ry be to God! I am

all on Je-sus' side, On the al-ter sanc-ti-fied, To the
Spir-it's power and light, I am liv-ing day and night, In the
blood has brought me in To God's ho-li-ness so clean, Where there's
sanc-ti-fied to God By the pow-er of the blood, Now the

The Shepherd Calling His Sheep

1. He's on the mountain calling His sheep— in the wilderness calling His sheep— He is ev-'ry-where calling His sheep— Oh hear Him.— When you're weary, hungry and cold— He will take you to His
2. He's a shelter in the time of storm. He will keep you from all harm; Hear the shepherd calling His sheep, Oh hear Him.— By the gospel calling His sheep, By the conscience calling His
3. He died to save your souls, He now lives to make you whole; Hear the shepherd calling His sheep, Oh hear Him.— In holiness walk with God, He will carry all your

Words: R. C. Lawson

Draw Me, Dear Jesus

Words and Music: Gladstone T. Harewood, 1923

Words: Dorothy A. Thrupp, 1836

Death Hath No Terror

1. Death has no terrors for the blood-bought one, O glory hallelujah to the Lamb! The boasted vic't'ry of the grave is gone,
2. Our souls die daily to the world and sin, O glory hallelujah to the Lamb! By the Spirit's power as He dwells within,
3. We seek a city far beyond this vale, O glory hallelujah to the Lamb! Where joys celestial never, never fail,
4. We'll then press forward to the heav'nly land, O glory hallelujah to the Lamb! Nor mind the troubles met on ev'ry hand,
5. We'll rise some day just as our Saviour rose, O glory hallelujah to the Lamb! Till then shall death be but a calm repose.

CHORUS

O glory hallelujah to the Lamb! Jesus rose from the dead, Rose triumphant as He said, Snatched the vic't'ry from the grave, Rose again our souls to save, O glory hallelujah to the Lamb!

Words and Music: Charles P. Jones, 1901

Worthy is the Lamb

1. Jesus Christ my Savior, He has set me free;
2. He was wounded for my transgressions and my iniquities;
3. John saw him in Heaven, King of kings was He

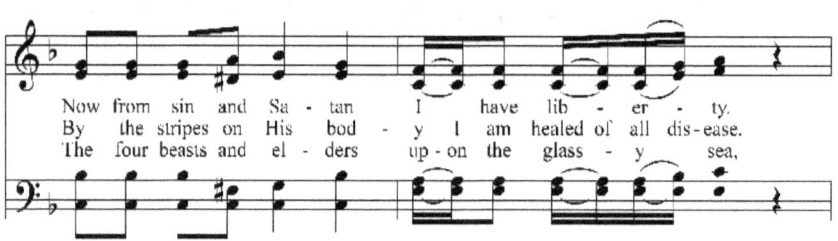

Now from sin and Satan I have liberty.
By the stripes on His body I am healed of all disease.
The four beasts and elders upon the glassy sea,

All because He loved me, Died upon the tree;
O, this great salvation makes me sing with glee
Threw their crowns before Him and fell down at His feet;

Died for my salvation on Mount Calvary.
In my heart I feel this is the year of Jubilee.
Crying worthy is the Lamb slain, to all eternity.

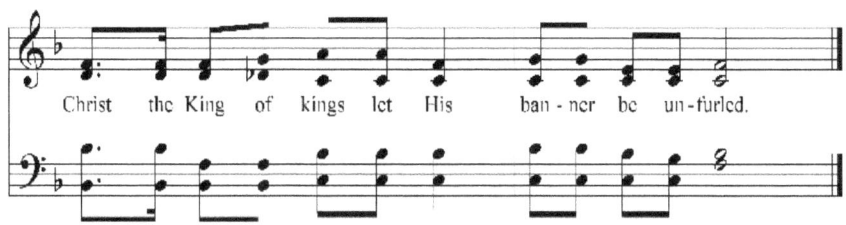

Words and Music: R. C. Lawson

Do You Know Him?

1. I know a man, From Galilee;
   If you're in sin I know He'll set you free.
2. He's the son of David, Seed of Abraham;
   Stone hewed out the mountain, He's the meek and humble lamb.
3. When you're in doubt, Fall on your knees;
   I know he'll hear and give your soul ease.
4. There's not a friend, So kind and true;
   He's ever ready, Yes, to carry you thru.
5. There's valleys so low, Mountains to climb;
   I have no fear because Jesus is mine.
6. Rivers so deep, Yes and so wide;
   But I know Jesus walks by my side,

Oh, Do you know Him?
Oh, Do you know Him?
Oh, Do you know Him?
Oh, Do you know Him?
Oh, Do you know Him?
Oh, Do you know Him?

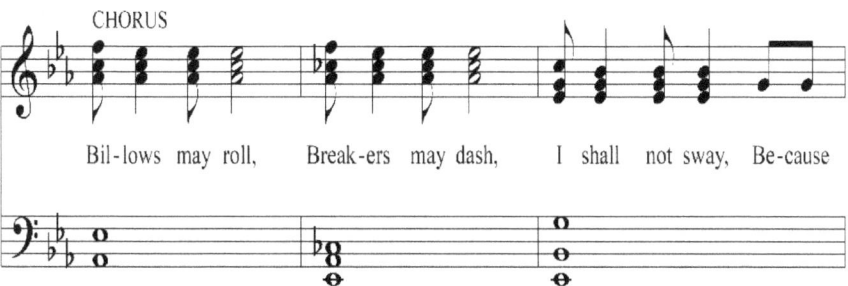

Words and Music: Mary Lou Parker

Words and Music: R. C. Lawson, 1924

Words: William H. Clark, 1854 – 1925

184

Let Jesus Fix It for You

1. If your life in days gone by, Has not been good and true,
2. Per-haps your tem-per is to blame, For man-y wrongs you do,
3. If in your home the troub-le is, The course you should per-sue,
4. And if some sin your soul hath bound With cords you can't un-do,
5. May-be to you the world is dark, And com-forts far and few,

In your own way no long-er try, But let Him fix it for you.
Take it to God in Je-sus' name, And He will fix it for you.
Go talk with God, your hand in His, And He will fix it for you.
At Je-sus' feet go lay it down, And He will fix it for you.
Let Je-sus own and rule your heart, And He will fix it for you.

CHORUS

Let Je-sus fix it for you, He knows just what to do;
When-ev-er you pray, let Him have His way, And He will fix it for you.

Words and Music: Charles A. Tindley, 1851-1933

185

It Is Well With My Soul

1. When peace, like a riv - er, at - tend - eth my way, When
2. Though Sa - tan should buf - fet, though tri - als should come, Let
3. My sin, oh, the bliss of this glo - ri - ous thought! My
4. For me, be it Christ, be it Christ hence to live: If
5. But, Lord, 'tis for Thee, for Thy com - ing we wait, The
6. And Lord, haste the day when my faith shall be sight, The

sor - rows like sea bil - lows roll; What - ev - er my lot, Thou has
this blest as - sur - ance con - trol, That Christ has re - gard - ed my
sin, not in part but the whole, Is nailed to the cross, and I
Jor - dan a - bove me shall roll, No pang shall be mine, for in
sky, not the grave, is our goal; Oh, trump of the an - gel! Oh,
clouds be rolled back as a scroll; The trump shall re - sound, and the

taught me to say, It is well, it is well, with my soul.
help - less es - tate, And hath shed His own blood for my soul.
bear it no more. Praise the Lord, praise the Lord, O my soul!
death as in life Thou wilt whis - per Thy peace to my soul.
voice of the Lord! Bless - ed hope, bless - ed rest of my soul.
Lord shall de - scend, E - ven so, it is well with my soul.

CHORUS

It is well, (it is well,) with my soul, (with my
soul,) It is well, it is well, with my soul.

Words: Horatio G. Spafford, 1873

Lead Me to Calvary

1. King of my life, I crown Thee now, Thine shall the glo-ry be;
   Lest I for-get Thy thorn-crowned brow, Lead me to Cal-va-ry.
2. Show me the tomb where Thou wast laid, Ten-der-ly mourned and wept;
   An-gels in robes of light ar-rayed Guard-ed Thee whilst Thou slept.
3. Let me like Ma-ry, through the gloom, Come with a gift to Thee;
   Show to me now the emp-ty tomb, Lead me to Cal-va-ry.
4. May I be will-ing, Lord, to bear Dai-ly my cross for Thee;
   E-ven Thy cup of grief to share, Thou hast borne all for me.

CHORUS
Lest I for-get Geth-sam-a-ne, Lest I for-get Thine ag-o-ny;
Lest I for-get Thy love for me, Lead me to Cal-va-ry.

Words: Jennie E. Hussey, 1874 - 1958

188

Love Lifted Me

1. In lov-ing-kind-ness Je-sus came, My soul in mer-cy to re-claim.
2. He called me long be-fore I heard, Be-fore my sin-ful heart was stirred;
3. His brow was pierced with man-y a thorn, His hand by cru-el nails were torn,
4. Now on a high-er plane I dwell, And with my soul I know 'tis well;

1. And from the depths of sin and shame Through grace He lift-ed me.
2. But when I took Him at His word, For-giv'n, He lift-ed me.
3. When from my guilt and grief, for-lorn, In love He lift-ed me.
4. Yet how or why, I can-not tell, He should have lift-ed me.

He lift-ed me.

CHORUS

From sink-ing sand He lift-ed me, With ten-der hand He lift-ed me;
From shades of night to plains of light, Oh, praise His Name, He lift-ed me!

Words and Music: Charles H. Gabriel, 1905

Words: William P. Mackay, 1863

Just As I Am

1. Just as I am, without one plea, But that Thy blood was shed for me, And that Thou bidst me come to Thee, O Lamb of God, I come, I come.
2. Just as I am, and waiting not To rid my soul of one dark blot, To Thee whose blood can cleanse each spot, O Lamb of God, I come, I come.
3. Just as I am, though tossed about With many a conflict, many a doubt, Fightings and fears within, without, O Lamb of God, I come, I come.
4. Just as I am, poor, wretched, blind; Sight, riches, healing of the mind, Yea, all I need in Thee to find, O Lamb of God, I come, I come.
5. Just as I am, Thou wilt receive, Wilt welcome, pardon, cleanse, relieve; Because Thy promise I believe, O Lamb of God, I come, I come.
6. Just as I am, Thy love unknown Hath broken ev'ry barrier down; Now, to be Thine, yea, Thine alone, O Lamb of God, I come, I come.

Words: Charlotte Elliott, 1835

Near the Cross

1. Jesus, keep me near the cross, There a precious fountain,
2. Near the cross, a trembling soul, Love and Mercy found me;
3. Near the cross! O Lamb of God, Bring its scenes before me;
4. Near the cross! I'll watch and wait Hoping, trusting ever,

Free to all, a healing stream Flows from Cal-v'ry's mountain.
There the bright and morning star Sheds its beams around me.
Help me walk from day to day, With its shadows o'er me.
Till I reach the golden strand, Just beyond the river.

CHORUS

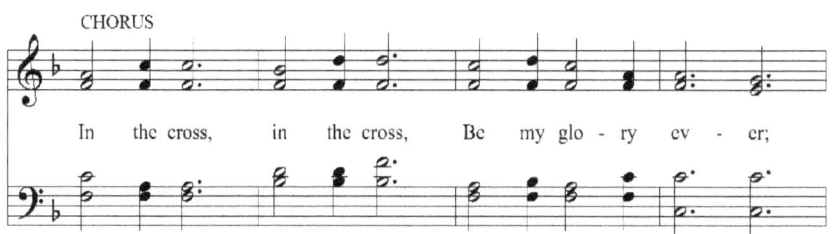

In the cross, in the cross, Be my glory ever;

Till my raptured soul shall find Rest beyond the river.

Words: Fannie J. Crosby, 1869

He Was Nailed to the Cross

1. What a wonderful, wonderful Savior, Who would die on the cross for me! Freely shedding His precious lifeblood, That the sinner might be made free.
2. Thus He left His heavenly glory, To accomplish His Father's plan; He was born of the virgin Mary, Took upon Him the form of man.
3. He was wounded for our transgressions, And He carried our sorrows, too; He's the Healer of ev'ry sickness, This He came to the world to do.
4. So He gave His life for others In Redeeming this world from sin, And He's gone to prepare a mansion, That at last we may enter in.

CHORUS

He was nailed to the cross for me, He was nailed to the cross for me; He was nailed to the cross, He was nailed to the cross, On the cross crucified for me He died; He was nailed to the cross for me.

Words and Music: Frederick A. Graves, 1906

Kneel at the Cross

1. Kneel at the cross, Christ will meet you there, Come while He waits for you;
   List to His voice, Leave with Him your care And be-gin life a-new.
2. Kneel at the cross, There is room for all Who would His glo-ry share;
   Bliss there a-waits, Harm can ne'er be-fall Those who are an-chored there.
3. Kneel at the cross, Give your i-dols up, Look un-to realms a-bove;
   Turn not a-way To life's spark-ling cup, Trust on-ly in His love.

CHORUS

Kneel at the cross, Leave ev-'ry care;
Kneel at the cross, Kneel at the cross, Leave ev-'ry care Leave ev-'ry care;
Kneel at the cross Je-sus will meet you there.
Kneel at the cross, Kneel at the cross, meet you there.

Words and Music: Charles E. Moody, 1924

195

Words: C. B. Widmeyer
Words: Joseph H. Gilmore, 1834 - 1918

The Haven of Rest

1. My soul in sad exile was out on life's sea, So burdened with sin and distressed, Till I heard a sweet voice, saying, "Make Me your choice": And I entered the "Haven of Rest"!

2. I yielded myself to His tender embrace, In faith taking hold of the Word, My fetters fell off, and I anchored my soul; The "Haven of Rest" is my Lord.

3. The song of my soul, since the Lord made me whole, Has been the old story so blest, Of Jesus, who'll save whosoever will have A home in the "Haven of Rest."

4. How precious the thought that we all may recline, Like John, the beloved so blest, On Jesus' strong arm, where no tempest can harm, Secure in the "Haven of Rest."

5. Oh, come to the Savior, He patiently waits To save by His power divine; Come, anchor your soul in the "Haven of Rest," And say, "My Beloved is mine."

Words: Henry L. Gilmour, 1890

198

He Hideth My Soul

199

Words: Fannie J. Crosby, 1820 - 1915

200

I Am Determined to Hold Out

1. When I first found Je - sus, some-thing o'er me stole, Like light-ning it went through me, and glo - ry filled my soul; Sal - va - tion made me hap - py, and took my fears a - way, And when I meet old Sa - tan, to him I al - ways say:
2. Sa - tan, he was an - gry, said he'd soon be back; Just let the path get nar - row, and he will lose the track; But I'm so full of glo - ry, my Lord I al - ways find, And I just say to Sa - tan, "Old man, get thee be - hind."
3. This old - time re - li - gion makes me some-times shout, I don't have time to gos - sip, nor an - y time to pout; They say that I'm too nois - y, but when these bless - ings flow, I shout, O hal - le - lu - jah, I want the world to know.
4. When I hear the trum - pet sound - ing in the sky, And see the moun-tains tremb - ling, to Heav - en I will fly; For Je - sus will be call - ing, there'll be no time to mend, With joy I'll go up sing - ing, "I've held out to the end."

201

Words and Music: C. S. & T. P. Hamilton, 1900

204

Farther Along

1. Tempt-ed and tried we're oft made to won-der Why it should be thus all the day long, While there are oth-ers liv-ing a-bout us, Nev-er mo-lest-ed tho in the wrong.
2. When death has come and tak-en our loved ones, It leaves our home so lone-ly and drear; Then do we won-der why oth-ers pros-per, Liv-ing so wick-ed year af-ter year.
3. Faith-ful till death said our lov-ing Mas-ter, A few more days to la-bor and wait; Toils of the road will then seem as noth-ing, As we sweep thru the beau-ti-ful gate.
4. When we see Je-sus com-ing in glo-ry, When He comes from His home in the sky; Then we shall meet Him in the bright man-sion, We'll un-der-stand it all by and by.

CHORUS
Far-ther a-long we'll know all a-bout it, Far-ther a-long we'll un-der-stand why; Cheer up, my broth-er, live in the sun-shine, We'll un-der-stand it all by and by.

Words and Music: W. B. Stevens, 1937

We Have an Anchor

1. Will your anchor hold in the storms of life, When the clouds unfold their wings of strife? When the strong tides lift, and the cables strain, Will your anchor drift, or firm remain?

2. It is safely moored, 'twill the storm withstand, For 'tis well secured by the Savior's hand; Though the tempest rage and the wild winds blow, Not an angry wave shall our bark o'er-flow.

3. When our eyes behold through the gath'ring night The city of gold, our harbor bright; We shall anchor fast by the heav'nly shore, With the storms all past for evermore.

CHORUS
We have an anchor that keeps the soul Steadfast and sure while the billows roll, Fastened to the Rock which cannot move, Grounded firm and deep in the Savior's love.

Words: Priscilla J. Owens, 1882

208

Take the Name of Jesus with You

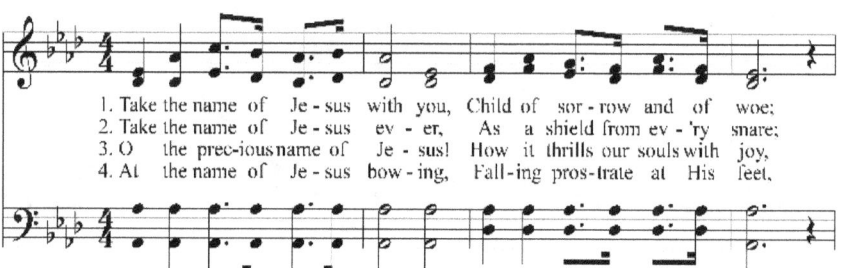

1. Take the name of Je-sus with you, Child of sor-row and of woe;
2. Take the name of Je-sus ev - er, As a shield from ev - 'ry snare;
3. O the prec-ious name of Je - sus! How it thrills our souls with joy,
4. At the name of Je-sus bow-ing, Fall-ing pros-trate at His feet,

It will joy and com - fort give you, Take it, then, wher - e'er you go.
If temp - ta - tions round you gath - er, Breathe that ho - ly name in prayer.
When His lov - ing arms re - ceive us, And His songs our tongues em - ploy!
King of kings in heav'n we'll crown Him, When our jour - ney is com - plete.

CHORUS

Prec-ious name, Oh how sweet! Hope of earth and joy of heav'n;
Prec-ious name, O how sweet!

Prec-ious name, O how sweet! Hope of earth and joy of heav'n.
Prec-ious name, O how sweet, how sweet!

Words: Lydia O. Baxter, 1870

My Savior First of All

Words: Fannie J. Crosby, 1891

More About Jesus

1. More about Jesus I would know, More of His grace to others show;
2. More about Jesus let me learn, More of His holy will discern;
3. More about Jesus, in His Word, Holding communion with my Lord;
4. More about Jesus on His throne, Riches in glory all His own;

More of His saving fulness see, More of His love who died for me.
Spirit of God, my teacher be, Showing the things of Christ to me.
Hearing His voice in ev'ry line, Making each faithful saying mine.
More of His kingdom's sure increase; More of His coming, Prince of Peace.

CHORUS

More, more about Jesus, More, more about Jesus;
More of His saving fulness see, More of His love who died for me.

Words: Eliza E. Hewitt, 1887

212

Words and Music: Lucie E. Campbell

I Walk With the King

1. In sorrow I wandered, my spirit oppressed, But now I am happy—securely I rest; From morning till evening glad carols I sing, And this is the reason I walk with the King.
2. For years in the fetters of sin I was bound, The world could not help me— no comfort I found; But now like the birds and the sunbeams of spring, I'm free and rejoicing I walk with the King.
3. O soul near despair in the lowlands of strife, Look up and let Jesus come into your life; The joy of salvation to you He would bring Come into the sunlight and walk with the King.

CHORUS
I walk with the King, hallelujah! I walk with the King, praise His name! No longer I roam, my soul faces home, I walk and I talk with the King.

Words: James Rowe, 1913

Wonderful Peace

1. Far away in the depths of my spirit to-night Rolls a melody sweeter than psalm; In celestial-like strains it unceasingly falls O'er my soul like an infinite calm.
2. What a treasure I have in this wonderful peace, Buried deep in the heart of my soul; So secure that no power can mine it away, While the years of eternity roll.
3. I am resting to-night in this wonderful peace, Resting sweetly in Jesus' control; For I'm kept from all danger by night and by day, And His glory is flooding my soul.
4. And methinks when I rise to that City of peace, Where the Author of peace I shall see, The one strain of the song which the ransomed will sing, In the heavenly kingdom shall be:
5. Ah! soul, are you here without comfort or rest, Marching down the rough pathway of time? Make Jesus your friend ere the shadows grow dark; Oh, accept this sweet peace so sublime.

CHORUS

Peace! Peace! Wonderful peace, Coming down from the Father above; Sweep over my spirit forever I pray, In fathomless billows of love.

Words: Warren D. Cornell, 1889

216

I Need Thee Every Hour
Words: Annie S. Hawks, 1872

1. I need Thee ev-'ry hour, most gra - cious Lord;
2. I need Thee ev-'ry hour, stay Thou near - by;
3. I need Thee ev-'ry hour, in joy or pain;
4. I need Thee ev-'ry hour, teach me Thy will;
5. I need Thee ev-'ry hour, most Ho - ly One;

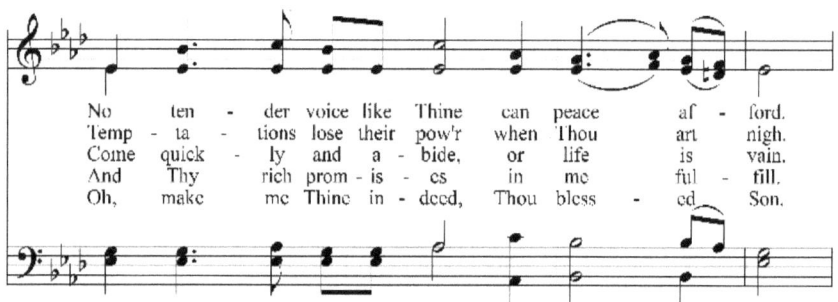

No ten - der voice like Thine can peace af - ford.
Temp - ta - tions lose their pow'r when Thou art nigh.
Come quick - ly and a - bide, or life is vain.
And Thy rich prom - is - es in me ful - fill.
Oh, make me Thine in - deed, Thou bless - ed Son.

CHORUS

I need Thee, oh, I need Thee; Ev - 'ry hour I need Thee;

Oh, bless me now, my Sav - ior, I come to Thee.

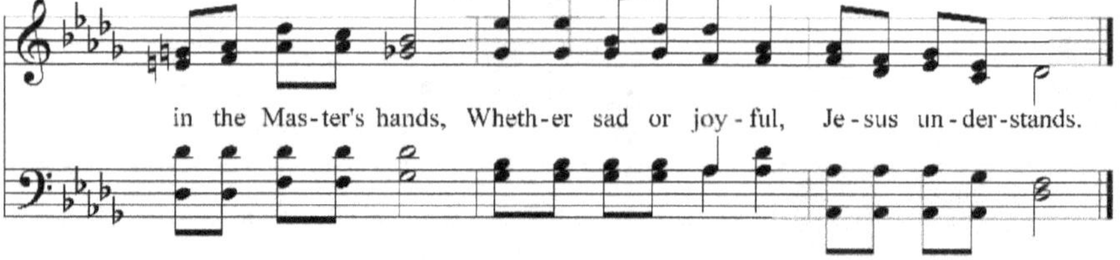

218

in the Mas-ter's hands, Wheth-er sad or joy-ful, Je-sus un-der-stands.

Jesus, Savior, Pilot Me

1. Je - sus, Sav - ior, pi - lot me, O - ver life's tem - pes - tuous sea;
2. As a moth - er stills her child, Thou canst hush the o - cean wild;
3. When at last I near the shore, And the fear - ful break - ers roar

Un - known waves be - fore me roll, Hid - ing rock and treach-'rous shoal;
Bois - t'rous waves o - bey Thy will When Thou say'st to them, "Be still!"
'Twixt me and the peace - ful rest, Then, while lean - ing on Thy breast,

Chart and com - pass came from Thee: Je - sus, Sav - ior, pi - lot me.
Won - drous Sov - 'reign of _ the sea, Je - sus, Sav - ior, pi - lot me.
May I hear Thee say to me, "Fear not, I will pi - lot thee."

Words: Edward Hopper, 1871

The Way of the Cross Leads Home

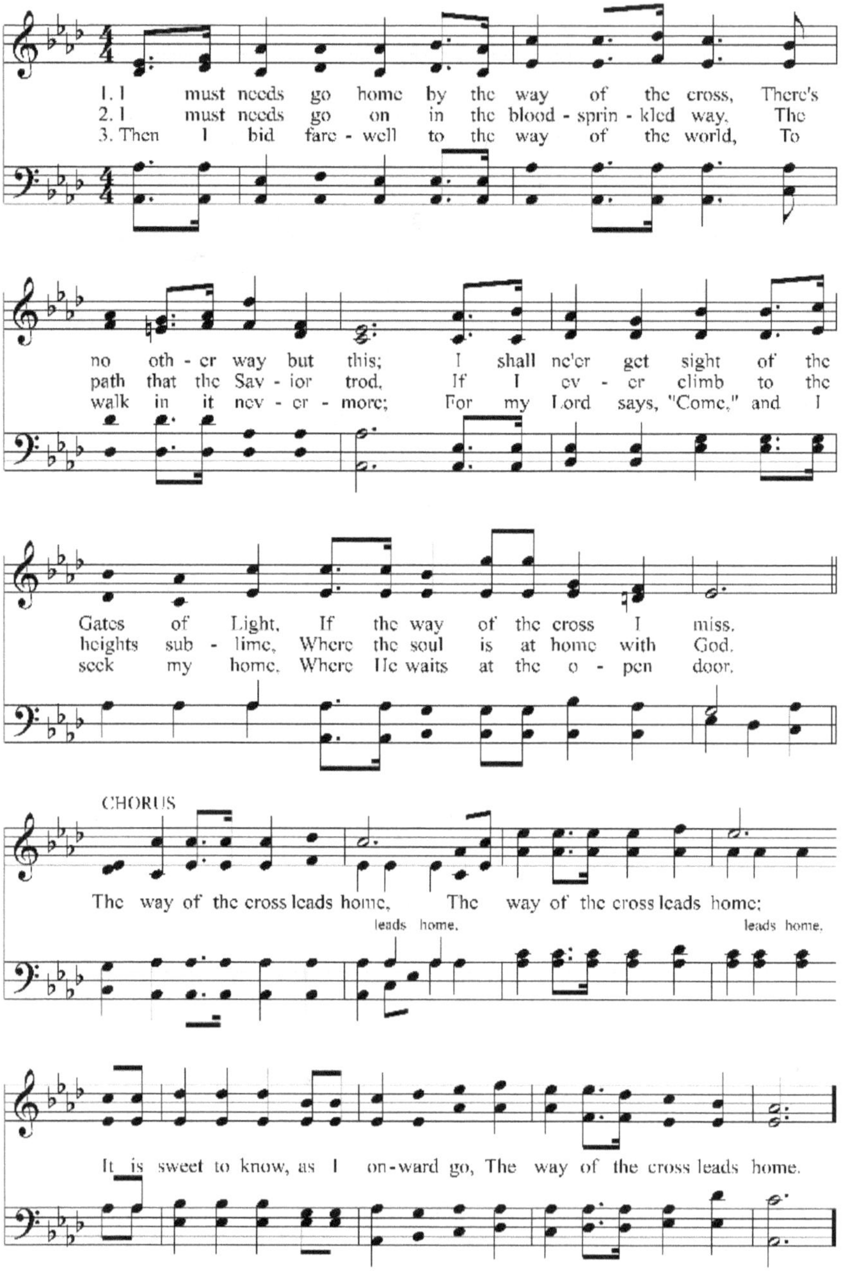
1. I must needs go home by the way of the cross, There's no oth - er way but this; I shall ne'er get sight of the Gates of Light, If the way of the cross I miss.
2. I must needs go on in the blood - sprin - kled way, The path that the Sav - ior trod, If I ev - er climb to the heights sub - lime, Where the soul is at home with God.
3. Then I bid fare - well to the way of the world, To walk in it nev - er - more; For my Lord says, "Come," and I seek my home, Where He waits at the o - pen door.
CHORUS
The way of the cross leads home, The way of the cross leads home;
leads home, leads home,
It is sweet to know, as I on-ward go, The way of the cross leads home.

Words: Jessie B. Pounds, 1906

Sweeter as the Years Go By

1. Of Jesus' love that sought me, When I was lost in sin;
2. He trod in old Judea Life's pathway long ago;
3. 'Twas wond-rous love which led Him For us to suffer loss—

Of wond-rous grace that brought me Back to His fold again;
The people thronged about Him, His saving grace to know;
To bear without a murmur The anguish of the cross;

Of heights and depths of mercy, Far deeper than the sea,
He healed the broken-hearted, And caused the blind to see;
With saints redeemed in glory, Let us our voices raise,

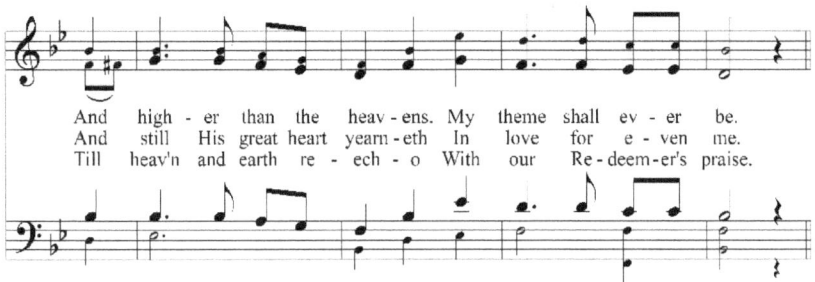

And higher than the heav-ens. My theme shall ever be.
And still His great heart yearn-eth In love for even me.
Till heav'n and earth re-ech-o With our Redeemer's praise.

222

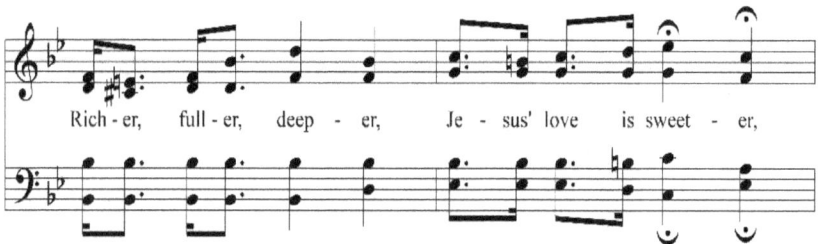

Words and Music: Leila N. Morris, © 1970, renewed 1998 Lillenas Publishing Company

In the Service of the King

1. I am hap-py in the serv-ice of the King, I am hap-py, oh, so hap-py; I have peace and joy that noth-ing else can bring, In the serv-ice of the King.
2. I am hap-py in the serv-ice of the King, I am hap-py, oh, so hap-py; Thro' the sun-shine and the shad-ow I can sing, In the serv-ice of the King.
3. I am hap-py in the serv-ice of the King, I am hap-py, oh, so hap-py; To His guid-ing hand for-ev-er I will cling, In the serv-ice of the King.
4. I am hap-py in the serv-ice of the King, I am hap-py, oh, so hap-py; All that I poss-ess to Him I glad-ly bring, In the serv-ice of the King.

CHORUS
In the serv-ice of the King, Ev-'ry tal-ent I will bring; I have peace and joy and bless-ing in the serv-ice of the King.

Words: Alfred H. Ackley, 1912

All the Way My Savior Leads Me

1. All the way My Sav-ior leads me, What have I to ask be-side?
Can I doubt His ten-der mer-cy, Who through life has been my Guide?
Heav'n-ly peace, di-vin-est com-fort, Here by faith in Him to dwell!
For I know, what-e'er be-fall me, Je-sus do-eth all things well;
For I know, what-e'er be-fall me, Je-sus do-eth all things well.

2. All the way my Sav-ior leads me, Cheers each wind-ing path I tread,
Gives me grace for ev-'ry tri-al, Feeds me with the liv-ing Bread.
Through my wear-y steps may fal-ter And my soul a thirst may be,
Gush-ing from the Rock be-fore me, Lo! A spring of joy I see;
Gush-ing from the Rock be-fore me, Lo! A spring of joy I see.

3. All the way my Sav-ior leads me, Oh, the full-ness of His love!
Per-fect rest to me is prom-ised In my Fath-er's house a-bove.
When my spir-it, clothed im-mor-tal, Wings its flight to realms of day
This my song through end-less a-ges: Je-sus led me all the way;
This my song through end-less a-ges: Je-sus led me all the way.

Words: Fannie J. Crosby, 1820 - 1915

Look to the Lamb of God

1. If you from sin are long-ing to be free, Look to the Lamb of God;
   He, to re-deem you, died on Cal-va-ry, Look to the Lamb of God.
2. When Sa-tan tempts, and doubts and fears as-sail, Look to the Lamb of God;
   You in His strength shall o-ver all pre-vail, Look of the Lamb of God.
3. Are you a-wea-ry, does the way seem long? Look to the Lamb of God;
   His love will cheer and fill your heart with song, Look to the Lamb of God.
4. Fear not when shad-ows on your path-way fall, Look to the Lamb of God;
   In joy or sor-row Christ is all in all, Look to the Lamb of God.

CHORUS
Look to the Lamb of God, Look to the Lamb of God,
the Lamb of God, the Lamb of God,
For He a-lone is a-ble to save you; Look to the Lamb of God.

Words: Henry G. Jackson, 1838 – 1914

Woke Up This Morning with My Mind

2. Can't hate your neighbor in your mind, if you keep it stayed, . . .
3. Makes you love everybody with your mind, when you keep it stayed, . . .
4. The devil can't catch you in your mind, if you keep it stayed, . . .
5. Jesus is the captain in your mind, when you keep it stayed, . . .

Words: Anonymous

Heavenly Sunlight

1. Walking in sunlight, all of my journey; Over the mountains, through the deep vale: Jesus has said "I'll never forsake thee," Promise divine that never can fail.
2. Shadows around me, shadows above me, Never conceal my Savior and Guide: He is the light, in Him is no darkness; Ever I'm walking close to His side.
3. In the bright sunlight, ever rejoicing, Pressing my way to mansions above; Singing His praises gladly I'm walking, Walking in sunlight, sunlight of love.

CHORUS
Heavenly sunlight, heavenly sunlight, Flooding my soul with glory divine: Hallelujah, I am rejoicing, Singing His praises, Jesus is mine.

Words: H. J. Zelley, 1859-1942

Almost Persuaded

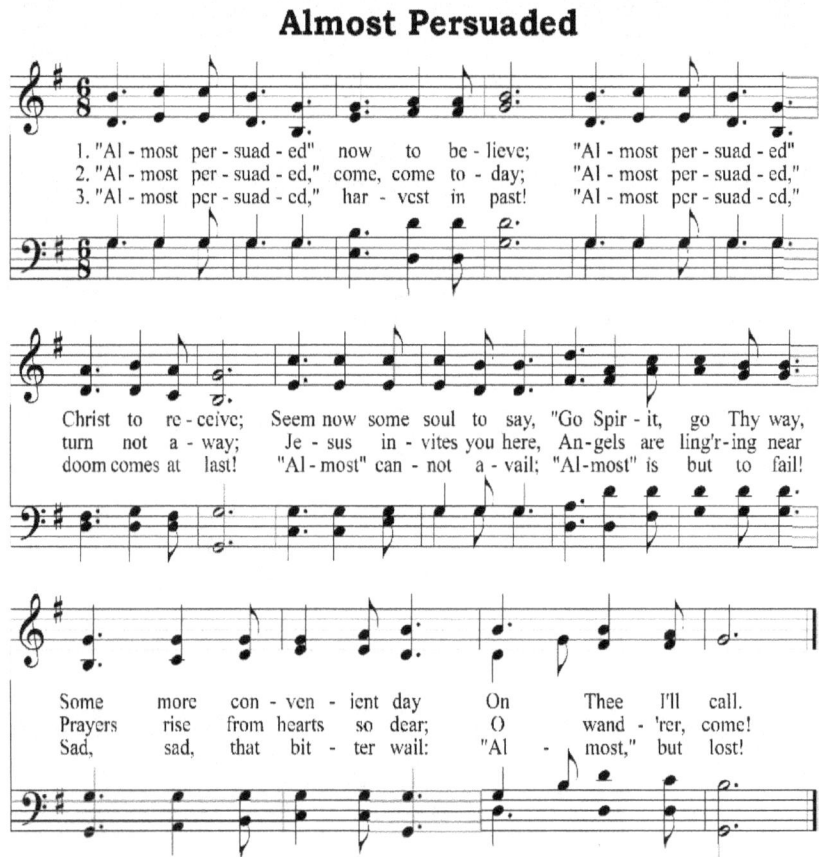

Words and Music: Philip P. Bliss, 1871

Words: William Williams, 1717-1791

I Love Jesus Best of All

1. I love to sing and pray, rejoicing ev-'ry day, I love the blessings when the showers on us fall, I love the fellowship within the narrow way, But I love Jesus best of all.
2. I love to testify of all He's done for me, I love to see the lost uplifted from the fall, I love to see them turn from all iniquity, But I love Jesus best of all.
3. I love to see the signs that follow saints of God, I love to hear the joy-bells ringing in my soul, I love to know He leads me by His staff and rod, But I love Jesus best of all.

CHORUS
For He saves my soul from sin, (from all my sin,) Gives me peace and joy within; (and makes me clean;) I've been buried in His name and of Him I'm not ashamed, For I love Jesus best of all.

Words and Music: Gladstone T. Harewood, 1924

235

Even Me

1. Lord I hear of show'rs of blessing,
2. Pass me not, O gentle Savior,
3. Bread of heav-en, bread of heav-en,

Thou art scat-t'ring full and free;
Sin-ful tho' my heart may be;
Ev-er let me feed on Thee;

Show'rs the thirst-y souls re-fresh-ing,
I am long-ing for Thy fa-vor,
Vine of heav-en, Vine of heav-en,

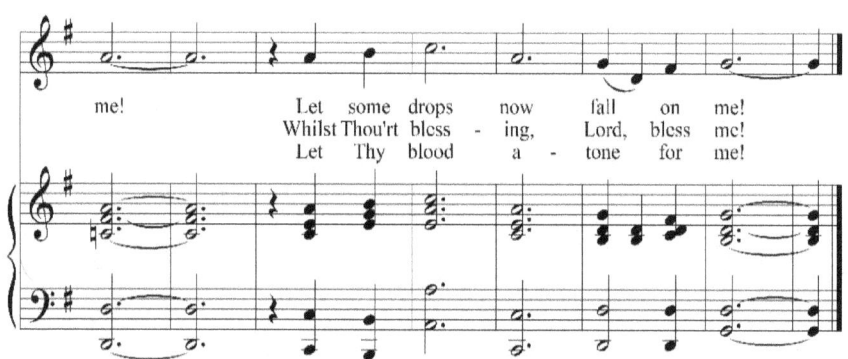

Words: Elizabeth H. Codner, 1824 – 1919

Joy Unspeakable

Words and Music: Barney E. Warren, 1900

His Eye Is on the Sparrow

1. Why should I feel discouraged, Why should the shadows come,
2. "Let not your heart be troubled," His tender word I hear,
3. Whenever I am tempted, Whenever clouds arise,

Why should my heart be lonely And long for heav'n and home,
And resting on His goodness, I lose my doubts and fears;
When songs give place to sighing, When hope within me dies,

When Jesus is my portion? My constant Friend is He: His
Tho' by the path He leadeth, But one step I may see: His
I draw the closer to Him, From care He sets me free; His

Words: Civilla D. Martin

That is Why I'm Going to Continue

I believe ev'ry word of God. I believe ev'ry word of God is true. I believe it is a shield to them who will put their trust in Him. I believe it shall forever stand, I believe it able to defend! I believe that all who live by Him shall reign with Christ our King.

Words and Music: Anonymous

243

I'm Going Through

1. Lord, I have start-ed to walk in the light That shines on my path-way so clear-ly, so bright; I've bade the world and its fol-lies a-dieu, And now with my Sav-ior I mean to go through.

2. Man-y once start-ed to run in this race, But with our Re-deem-er they could not keep pace; Oth-ers ac-cept-ed be-cause it was new, But not ver-y man-y seem bound to go through.

3. Let me but fol-low my Lord all a-lone, And have for my pil-low, like Ja-cob, a stone, Rath-er than vain world-ly pleas-ures pur-sue, Than turn from this path-way and fail to go through.

4. Come then, my com-rades, and walk in this way That leads to the king-dom of un-end-ing day; Turn from your i-dols and join with the few, Start in with your Sav-ior, and keep go-ing through.

Words and Music: Herbert Buffum, 1914

Leaning on the Everlasting Arms

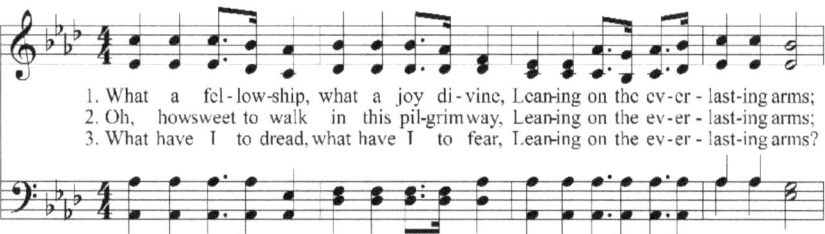

1. What a fel-low-ship, what a joy di-vine, Lean-ing on the ev-er-last-ing arms;
2. Oh, how sweet to walk in this pil-grim way, Lean-ing on the ev-er-last-ing arms;
3. What have I to dread, what have I to fear, Lean-ing on the ev-er-last-ing arms?

What a bless-ed-ness, what a peace is mine, Lean-ing on the ev-er-last-ing arms.
Oh, how bright the path grows from day to day, Lean-ing on the ev-er-last-ing arms.
I have bless-ed peace with my Lord so near, Lean-ing on the ev-er-last-ing arms.

CHORUS

Lean - ing, lean - ing, safe and se-cure from all a-larms;
Lean-ing on Je-sus, Lean-ing on Je-sus,

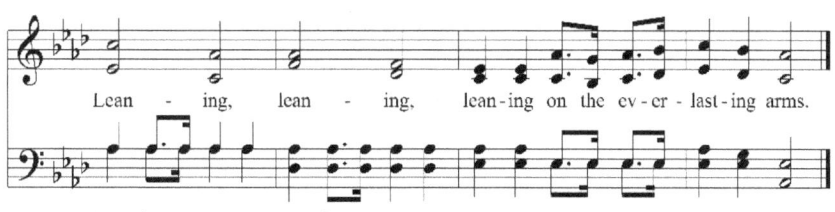

Lean - ing, lean - ing, lean-ing on the ev-er-last-ing arms.
Lean-ing on Je-sus, Lean-ing on Je-sus,

Words: Elisha A. Hoffman, 1887

O Master, Let Me Walk with Thee

1. O Master, let me walk with Thee
2. Help me the slow of heart to move
3. Teach me Thy patience! Still with Thee
4. In hope that sends a shining ray

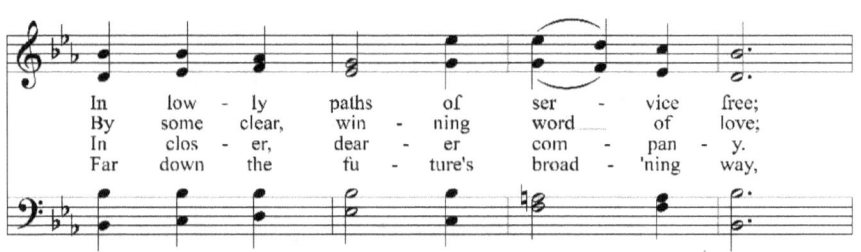

In lowly paths of service free;
By some clear, winning word of love;
In closer, dearer company.
Far down the future's broad'ning way,

Tell me Thy secret; help me bear The
Teach me the wayward feet to stay, And
In work that keeps faith sweet and strong, In
In peace that only Thou canst give, With

strain of toil, the fret of care.
guide them in the homeward way.
trust that triumphs over wrong.
Thee, O Master, let me live.

Words: Washington Gladden, 1879

247

Master, the Tempest Is Raging

1. Master, the tempest is raging! The billows are tossing high! The sky is o'er shadowed with blackness, No shelter or help is nigh; "Carest Thou not that we perish?" How canst Thou lie asleep, When each moment so madly is threat'ning, A grave in the angry deep?

2. Master, with anguish of spirit I bow in my grief today; The depths of my sad heart are troubled; O waken and save, I pray! Torrents of sin and of anguish Sweep o'er my sinking soul! And I perish! I perish, dear Master; O hasten, and take control!

3. Master, the terror is over, The elements sweetly rest; Earth's sun in the calm lake is mirrored, And heaven's within my breast. Linger, O blessed Redeemer, Leave me alone no more; And with joy I shall make the blest harbor, And rest on the blissful shore.

248

Words: Mary A. Baker
Music: Horatius R. Palmer, 1874

Words: Ludie D. Pickett,

250

251

Joy to the World

1. Joy to the world! the Lord is come; Let earth re-ceive her King; Let ev-'ry heart pre-pare Him room, And heav'n and na-ture sing, And heav'n and na-ture sing, And heav'n, and heav'n and na-ture sing.
2. Joy to the world! the Sav-ior reigns; Let men their songs em-ploy; While fields and floods, rocks, hills, and plains Re-peat the sound-ing joy, Re-peat the sound-ing joy, Re-peat, re-peat, the sound-ing joy.
3. No more let sins and sor-rows grow, Nor thorns in-fest the ground; He comes to make His bless-ings flow Far as the curse is found, Far as the curse is found, Far as, far as the curse is found.
4. He rules the world with truth and grace, And makes the na-tions prove The glo-ries of His right-eous-ness, And won-ders of His love, And won-ders of His love, And won-ders, and won-ders of His love.

Words and Music: Isaac Watts, 1719

252

Come, All Ye Faithful

1. O come, all ye faithful, joyful and triumphant,
2. Sing, choirs of angels, sing in exultation,
3. Yea, Lord, we greet Thee, born this happy morning,

O come, ye, O come ye to Bethlehem;
O sing, all ye bright hosts of heav'n above;
Jesus, to Thee be all glory giv'n;

Come and behold Him born the King of angels;
Glory to God, all glory in the highest;
Word of the Father, now in flesh appearing;

CHORUS

O come, let us adore Him, O come, let us adore Him,

O come, let us adore Him, Christ the Lord.

Words: John F. Wade, 1743

The Old Rugged Cross

1. On a hill far a-way stood an old rug-ged cross, The
2. O that old rug-ged cross, so des-pised by the world, Has a
3. In the old rug-ged cross, stained with blood so di-vine, A
4. To the old rug-ged cross I will ev-er be true, Its

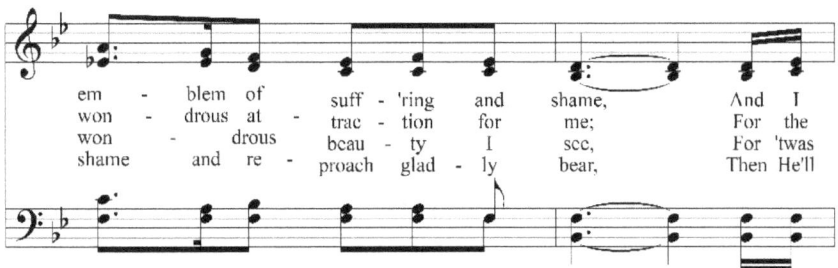

em-blem of suff-'ring and shame, And I
won-drous at-trac-tion for me; For the
won-drous beau-ty I see, For 'twas
shame and re-proach glad-ly bear, Then He'll

love that old cross where the dear-est and best For a
dear Lamb of God left His glo-ry a-bove, To
on that old cross Je-sus suf-fered and died, To
call me some-day to my home far a-way, Where His

world of lost sin-ners was slain.
bear it to dark Cal-va-ry.
par-don and sanc-ti-fy me.
glo-ry for-ev-er I'll share.

Words and Music: George Bennard, 1913

When The Battle's Over

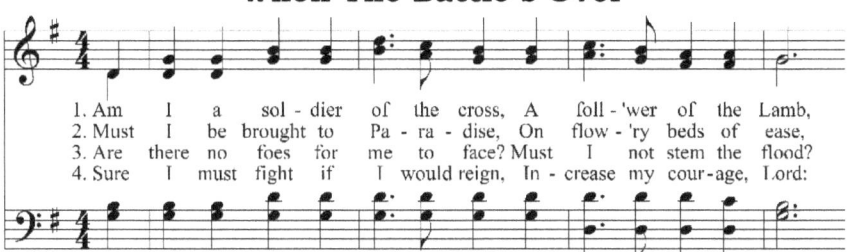

1. Am I a soldier of the cross, A foll-'wer of the Lamb,
2. Must I be brought to Paradise, On flow-'ry beds of ease,
3. Are there no foes for me to face? Must I not stem the flood?
4. Sure I must fight if I would reign, Increase my courage, Lord:

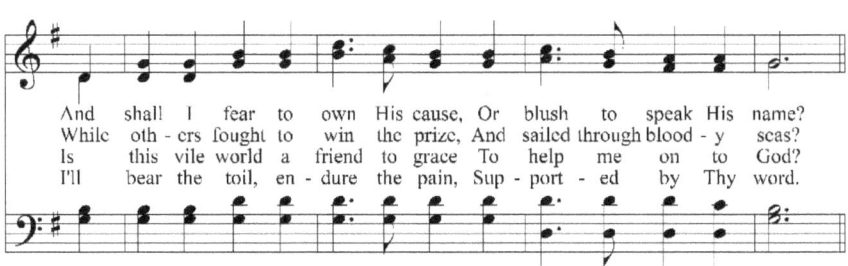

And shall I fear to own His cause, Or blush to speak His name?
While others fought to win the prize, And sailed through bloody seas?
Is this vile world a friend to grace To help me on to God?
I'll bear the toil, endure the pain, Supported by Thy word.

CHORUS

And when the battle's over we shall wear a crown! Yes,

we shall wear a crown! Yes, we shall wear a crown! And when the battle's

256

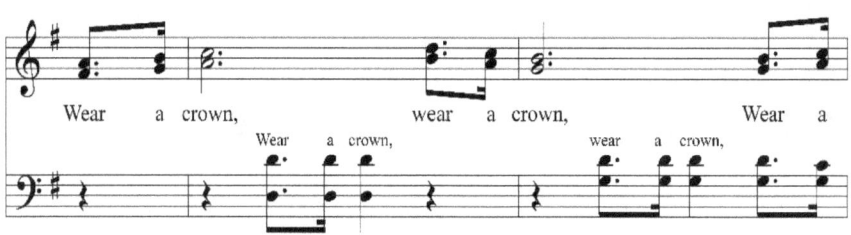

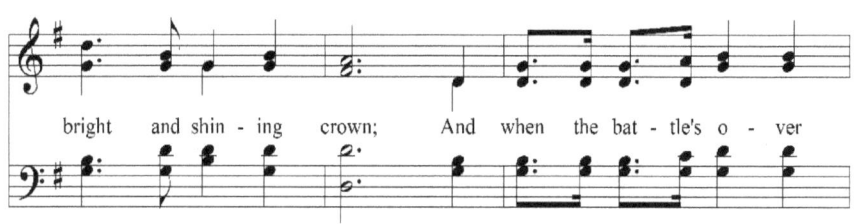

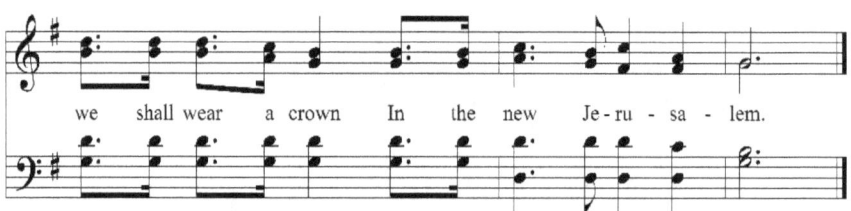

Words and Music: Isaac Watts

God Be With You

1. God be with you till we meet again! By His counsel's guide, uphold you, With His sheep securely fold you; God be with you till we meet again!
2. God be with you till we meet again! 'Neath His wings securely hide you, Daily manna still provide you; God be with you till we meet again!
3. God be with you till we meet again! Keep love's banner floating o'er you, Smite death's threat'ning wave before you; God be with you till we meet again!

CHORUS
Till we meet! Till we meet! Till we meet at Jesus' feet; Till we meet! Till we meet! Till we meet! God be with you till we meet again!

Words: William G. Tomer, 1833 - 1896

258

Since Jesus Came into My Heart

1. What a won-der-ful change in my life has been wrought Since Je-sus came in-to my heart; I have light in my soul for which long I have sought, Since Je-sus came in-to my heart.
2. I have ceased from my wand-'ring and go-ing a-stray, Since Je-sus came in-to my heart; And my sins which were man-y are all washed a-way, Since Je-sus came in-to my heart.
3. I'm pos-sessed of a hope that is stead-fast and sure, Since Je-sus came in-to my heart; And no dark clouds of doubt now my path-way ob-scure; Since Je-sus came in-to my heart.
4. There's a light in the val-ley of death now for me, Since Je-sus came in-to my heart; And the gates of the Cit-y be-yond I can see, Since Je-sus came in-to my heart.
5. I shall go there to dwell in that Cit-y I know, Since Je-sus came in-to my heart; And I'm hap-py, so hap-py as on-ward I go, Since Je-sus came in-to my heart.

Since Je-sus came in-to my heart, Since Je-sus came in-to my heart; Floods of joy o'er my soul like the sea bil-lows roll, Since Je-sus came in-to my heart.

Words: Rufus H. McDaniel, 1914

Give Me a Clean Heart

Words: Margaret J. Douroux
Music: Albert Denis Tessier

The Author and the Finisher

1. He's the Auth-or and the Fin-ish-er, Be-gin-ning and the End, All God's prom-is-es in Him are yea; He is Al-pha and O-me-ga, and He is the great A-men, Tak-ing all our sins a-way.

2. He's the Lamb of God, the King of kings, the bright and morn-ing Star, And the Shep-herd of the sheep is He; He's the might-y God, the Lord of hosts, the bless-ed Prince of peace, Un-to all e-ter-nit-y.

CHORUS
So we will love Him, we will trust Him, His word we will o-bey, In the wa-ter we'll be bur-ied in His name; the name of Je-sus; We will serve our Lord and Mas-ter ev-'ry pass-ing day And the rich-es of His grace pro-claim.

Words and Music: A. R. Schooler, 1920

262

Sweet Hour of Prayer

1. Sweet hour of prayer, sweet hour of prayer, That calls me from a world of care,
2. Sweet hour of prayer, sweet hour of prayer, The joys I feel, the bliss I share
3. Sweet hour of prayer, sweet hour of prayer, Thy wings shall my pe - ti - tion bear

And bids me at my Fath-er's throne, Make all my wants and wish-es known!
Of those whose an-xious spir-its burn With strong de-sires for thy re-turn!
To Him, whose truth and faith-ful-ness En - gage the wait-ing soul to bless:

In sea-sons of dis-tress and grief, My soul has of-ten found re-lief,
With such I has-ten to the place, Where God my Sav-ior shows His face,
And since He bids me seek His face, Be-lieve His Word, and trust His grace,

And oft es-caped the tempt-er's snare By thy re-turn, sweet hour of prayer.
And glad-ly take my sta-tion there, And wait for thee, sweet hour of prayer.
I'll cast on Him my ev-'ry care, And wait for thee, sweet hour of prayer.

Words: William W. Walford, 1772 - 1850

Just A Little Talk With Jesus

I once was lost in sin but Jesus took me in
And then a little light from heaven filled my soul
It bathed my heart in love and wrote my name above
And just a little talk with Jesus made me whole

Chorus
Now let us have a little talk with Jesus
Let us tell Him all about our troubles
He will hear our faintest cry
He will answer by and by
Now when you feel a little prayer wheel turning
And you know a little fire is burning
You will find a little talk with Jesus makes it right

Sometimes my path seems dreary without a ray of cheer
And then the cloud about me hides the light of day
The mists in me rise and hide the stormy skies
But just a little talk with Jesus clears the way

I may have doubts and fears, my eyes be filled with tears
But Jesus is a friend who watches day and night
I go to Him in prayer, He knows my every care
And just a little talk with Jesus makes it right

Words: Lister C. Derricks, 1937

All Alone

On Mt. Olive's sacred brow
Jesus spent the night in prayer
He is the pattern for us all, all alone
If we could only steal away
In some portion of the day
We will find it always pays to be alone

There are days to fast and pray
For the pilgrim in this way
There are days I like to be with Christ alone
We can tell Him our grief
He will give us quick relief
There are days I like to be with Christ alone

Chorus

There are days I like to be with Christ the Lord
I can tell Him all my troubles, all alone
There are days I like to be with Christ the Lord
I can tell Him all my troubles, all alone

Words: G. T. Byrd

Answer Him Lord I Will
Jesus is calling you to the light
Sweetly His accents thrill
While He is bidding you come tonight
Only say, Lord I will

Chorus
Only say, Lord I will, I will
Only say, Lord I will, I will
While He so tenderly bids you come
Answer Him Lord I will

Jesus is bidding you at His feet
All of your sins to lay
He will give pardon and peace complete
Taking your guilt away

Jesus invites you to come in faith
Laden with grief and blame
I will forgive you His dear voice saith
Trust in His saving name

Bid all your hindering doubts depart
Cling to Christ's promise still
While He is saying give me thine heart
Answer Him Lord I will
Words: Jennie Wilson

Jesus, I'll Never Forget

Jesus, I'll never forget, when away down in Egypt land
How you brought me out, with a mighty outstretched hand
Broke the bonds of sin, and set me free
Gave me joy, peace and liberty

Chorus

Jesus, I'll never forget what you've done for me
Jesus, I'll never forget how you set me free
Jesus, I'll never forget how you brought me out
Jesus, I'll never forget no, never

Jesus, I'll never forget how you stood by me
When I lost all help and was in misery
You strengthened my poor soul and bid me live
Now a consecrated life to Thee I'll give

I'm Saved

Some people wonder why we say
I'm Saved
I'm Saved
I'm Free
They want to know why we don't go
To the Dance
The answer's easy to be had
We are Saved

Chorus
It's Glory to know
I'm Saved
I'm Happy to tell
I'm Free
I once was Bound
With the chains of Sin
It's Victory
To Know I've Christ within

There's A Highway to Heaven
My way gets brighter
My load gets lighter
Walking up the King's highway
There's joy in knowing
With Him I'm going
Walking up the King's highway

Chorus
It's a highway to Heaven
None can walk up there but the pure in heart
It's a highway to Heaven
I am walking up the King's highway

Don't have to worry
Don't have to hurry
Walking up the King's highway
Christ walks beside me
Angels to guide me
Walking up the King's highway

If you're not walking
Start while I'm talking
Walking up the King's highway
There'll be a blessing
You'll be possessing
Walking up the King's highway

He Never Has Left Me Alone

Shadows may gather and strong clouds may roll
He never has left me alone
Dark waves of sorrow may sweep o'er my soul
He never has left me alone

Chorus

He never has left me alone
He never has left me alone
By night and by day He is with me alway
He never has left me alone

God is my refuge, my strength and my guide
He never has left me alone
Under His wings I can safely abide
He never has left me alone

Satan may tempt me and friends may depart
He never has left me alone
I have his promise secure in my heart
He never has left me alone

Wonderful blessings God gives to me
He never has left me alone
Blessings un-numbered as sands of the sea
He never has left me alone

Caught Up to Meet Him

One day I'm going where Jesus is
One day I'm going where Jesus is
One day I'm going where Jesus is
I'll be caught up to meet Him in the air

Chorus
I'll be caught up to meet Him
Caught up to meet Him
Where joy, happiness, and peace abide
There we'll meet in glory and we'll tell the story
Pressing onward to glorious day

Jesus, He saved my soul one day
Jesus, He saved my soul one day
Jesus, He saved my soul one day
I'll be caught up to meet Him in the air

Oh bye – bye and bye I'm going for a chariot ride
Oh bye – bye and bye I'm going for a chariot ride

I'm Going Back to Jesus

I'm going back to Jesus, I can no longer wander
My heart I turned to Jesus. I cannot grieve Him longer
I miss the sweet communion, the peace of heavenly union
My heart is turned to Jesus and I must go

Chorus

I'm going back to Jesus (repeat)
I'm going where the living waters flow
I can hear my Savior calling. Repentance tears are falling
My heart is turned back to Jesus and I must go

I'm traveling back to Jesus. My steps are slow and feeble
I pray that the Lord will help me and keep me from all evil
And should my strength forsake me, dear Jesus come and take me
My heart is turned to Jesus, I must go

You Shall Wear a Golden Crown

Watch ye therefore ye know not the day
When the Lord shall call your soul away
If you labor striving for the right
You shall wear a golden crown

Chorus
Brethren, I shall wear a crown
When the trumpet sounds, "Yes"
I shall wear a crown, I shall
Wear a golden crown

Be not like the foolish virgins then
For He's coming and you know not when
Have your lamps all trimmed and burning bright
You shall wear a golden crown

Though the host of hell your soul assail
Naught of these against you shall prevail
Never faint nor lay thine armor down
And you shall wear a golden crown

Oh, the Joy that Came to Me
When my Savior found me
Put His arms around me
Whispered peace and made me free
How He walks beside me
To protect and guide me
Oh the joy that came to me

Chorus
Oh the joy that came to me
When I knew that I was free
When my Savior found me
Oh the joy that came to me

When I knew the story
Of the life in glory
When I heard of Calvary
And of how He pleaded
Just for what I needed
Oh the joy that came to me

Oh the supernatural of the life eternal
In the home beyond the sea
That awaits the lowly
Faithful pure and holy
Oh the joy that came to me

I Was Lost
Oh glory to the Lord, all my sins He took away
I was lost and Jesus found me
I was dead but now I live

Chorus
I was lost and Jesus found me
I was dead but now I live
Oh glory, glory, glory, to the "Great Eternal God"

My burden was too heavy
Day and night I could not rest
Then I heard Jesus saying
Come to me and you'll find rest

Then He brought me to the fold
And He cleansed my sins away
Filled my heart-with joy and peace
That no one can take away

Jesus all the glory I give
Slave I was He set me free
On Jesus' breast, now I rest
Earthly charms no more for me

Going On All I Know

The test is on everywhere I go
I have a little faith but I need some more

I'm going on, on, all I know
I'm going on, on, all I know
Going on, to that city
Where mansions are prepared for me

The Lord knew what I needed most
So He baptized me with the Holy Ghost

Of the word, I was not ashamed
I've been baptized in Jesus name

Now I'm saved and sanctified
Through His precious blood applied

Satan don't like it, but I'm saved from sin
By the Holy Ghost that dwells within

Oh, What's He Done for Me

Jesus loves me with unchanging love
He to save me left His house above
All my grief He bore upon the tree
I never could tell all He's done for me

Oh! What He has done for me
Oh! What He has done for me
If I tried through eternity
I never could tell what He's done for me

When I fell beneath a heavy load
Faint and weary on the downward road
Jesus took me from the miry clay
He led me into the King's Highway

I have sorrows hard to bear
Heavy burdens that none could share
When I faint in my bitter grief
He is the one that comes to my relief

I am so glad that Jesus is my friend
His friendship that will never end
Oh, that I could make the whole world see
Just what a Savior Jesus is to me

Never Draw Back
God shall be first in everything
No works of mine to Him I bring
Thro' grace I shall defeat the foe
A victor is this world of woe

Chorus
I will never draw back, but move along
I have said good-by to the careless throng
I will walk with Jesus, 'tis sweeter so
I will be a victor in this world of woe

Come loss or gain; let friends forsake
Come joy or pain, or martyr stake
With Jesus only let me go
A victor in this world of woe

Let heart be crushed and burdens fall
He will give grace to bear it all
With Jesus by my side, I go
A victor in this world of woe

No vulture's eye this patch can see
That God hath chosen here for me
Alone with Him 'tis sweet to know
He keeps me in this world of woe

That city and my home, sweet home
Lie just beyond the sunset foam
My sails are full and fair winds blow
To bear me from this world of woe

Yes, there is Power in His Name
What makes the virtue in the water?
It is in Jesus' name
It is in Jesus' name
What makes the devil fear and scatter?
It's the mighty power in His name

Chorus
Oh! Glory
Yes, there is power, yes, there is power
Yes, there is power in His name
All sickness must go
And the healing waters flow
I know there is power in His name

What words said Peter to the lame man?
He said, "In Jesus name"
He said, "In Jesus name"
"Rise up and walk," and then the same man
Found the wealth and power in His name

How should we ask of God a favor?
Ask in Jesus' name
Ask in Jesus' name
What gives us faith that will not waiver?
'Tis the Word when preached in Jesus' name

How should we baptize all believers?
Should be in Jesus name
Should be in Jesus name
No other is given to redeem them
For the power of redemption in His name

I Can Tell the World About This
Chorus
I can tell the world this
I can tell the nations I'm blessed
Tell them what Jesus has done
Tell them that the Comforter has come
And He brought joy, great joy to my soul

My Lord, He told Moses what to do
He did, my Lord. O yes, He did
To go lead the children of Israel through
Yes He did, my Lord. O yes He did
And He brought joy, joy, joy to my soul

My Lord done just what He said
Yes, He did, my Lord. O Yes, He did
He healed the sick and then He raised the dead
Yes He did, my Lord. O yes, He did
And He brought joy, joy, joy to my soul

My Lord, He rose up in the air
Yes He did, my Lord. O yes He did
And He called poor sinners from everywhere
Yes He did, my Lord. O yes He did
And He brought joy, joy, joy to my soul

Nobody But The Lord

Who healed my wounded heart one evening?
Nobody but You, Lord – nobody but you
Who stopped my poor weary heart from grieving?
Nobody but You, Lord – nobody but You

Chorus
Nobody but You, Lord – nobody but You
Can keep me Holy and living true
When I'm in trouble, You carry me through
Nobody but You, Lord – nobody but You

Who can calm the ocean's wildest billows?
Nobody but You, Lord – nobody but You
Who can make down life's death pillows?
Nobody but You, Lord – nobody but You

Who gives peace for every trail?
Nobody but You, Lord – nobody but You
Who gives me joy and no denial?
Nobody but You, Lord – nobody but You

Who died to save the world from sorrow?
Nobody but You, Lord – nobody but You
Who gives us power for tomorrow?
Nobody but You, Lord – nobody but You

Is Everybody Happy?
Down in the valley where the violets grow
I met a man who was meek and low
He's a friend that will never fail
A solid rock that will never quail
The devil is a lair from the world's begin
He says that we can't live free from sin
But I've been redeemed from the raging foe
And I don't have to sin no more

Chorus
Is everyone happy? Is everybody glad?
I don't want to see you looking wearied
I don't want to see you looking sad
I want to see you keep a' smiling
As if Jesus was at the door
Keep on a' shouting hallelujah
Until we meet on the other shore

Thou art fair, my beloved one. Thou art fair
Unto Thee whom can I compare?
Thou art unto me as a banner of love
Shining and gleaming as the stars above
Teach me the way that I shall go
That I may never walk in sin no more
For if I walk as I've once before
To me it's woe, woe, woe

On the hill called Calvary I can see
Where Jesus suffered and died for me
He walked the seashore of Galilee
The world would have never been reconciled
If Jesus had never suffered, bled and died
He's a friend and a friend indeed
Over this whole, wide world

I'm Going to Live the Life I Sing About in My Song

Every day, everywhere on the busy thoroughfare
Folks may watch me. Some may spot me
Say I'm foolish, but I don't care
I can't sing one thing and then live another
Be a saint by day and a devil under cover
I'm going to live the life I sing about in my song

Chorus

I'm going to live the life I sing about in my song
I'm going to stand for right and always shun the wrong
In the crowd or if I'm alone
On the streets or in my home
I'm going to live the life I sing about in my song

If at day, if at night, I must always walk in the light
Some mistake me, underrate me, because
I want to do what's right
I can't go to church and shout all day Sunday
Go get drunk and raise sand on Monday
I've got to live the life I sing about in my Song

Let's Go Back

In this modernistic day, we have strayed too far
away
From our camp meeting and praying ground
Where we would fast and pray all day and let
God have His way
Back there on the old praying ground

Chorus

Oh! Let's go back. Let's go back to our Father's
praying ground
God is not pleased. Let's go back on bended
knee
Too far away we have strayed
Just now and then a soul is saved
Let's go back to our Father's praying ground

Through the country they would ride
With their children by their side
Traveling through some cold, and rain, just the
same
Going to the house of the Lord, where they
would bow in one accord
Singing come ye that love the Lord in Jesus'
name

Though the preacher could hardly read
What he said, sinners took heed
And would steal away somewhere and bow down
Sometimes by an old tree
One would cry out, "He spoke peace to me
Just before, at my old praying ground"

I Am Out on the Battlefield

I was alone and idle. I was a sinner too
I heard a voice from Heaven saying, "There is work to do"
I took the Master's hand. Joined the Christian band
Now I am out on the battlefield for my Lord

I left my friends and kindred. I am bound for the Promised Land
The grace of God upon me, the Bible in my hand
In distant land I've trod crying, "Sinner come to God"
I am out on the battlefield for my Lord

I lost my flag in battle. The staff is in my hand
I'll take it to Jesus over in the glory land
And then the sun will shine in the little soul of mine
I am out on the battlefield for my Lord

Chorus

I am out on the battlefield for my Lord
Yes, I am out on the battlefield for my Lord
And I promised Him that I would serve Him till I die
I am out on the battlefield for my Lord

He's Got the Whole World in His Hand

Just come on with your money
Don't be afraid to give
He's got the whole world in His hand
He sure will let you live

Chorus
He's got the whole world in His hand
He's got the whole world in His hand
He's got the whole world in His hand
He's got the world in His hand

He just asks for a dime of a dollar
He'll bless you if you will
But in the free-will offering
He'll take whatever you give

The Holy Ghost is a teacher
Indeed He will make you wise
If you listen to His teachings
He will teach you to pay your tithes

Some say I give to the cripple
Some say I give to the blind
But when you get through giving
You owe the Lord that dime

What He Done For Me

He sanctified me with the Holy Ghost
What He done for me (Repeat twice)
I shall never forget what He done for me

Chorus

Oh, Oh, Oh, Oh, what He done for me (Repeat twice)
I never shall forget what He done for me

He took my feet out of miry clay
What He done for me (Repeat twice)
I never shall forget what He done for me

He baptized my soul with the Holy Ghost
What He done for me (Repeat twice)
I never shall forget what He done for me

Come and Go with Me
No confusion up there in My Father's house
In my Father's house, in my father's house
There's no confusion up there in my Father's house
There is peace, peace, peace

Chorus
Come and go with me to my Father's house
To my Father's house, to my Father's house
Come and go with me to my Father's house
There is peace, peace, peace

Joy and peace over there in my Father's house
In my Father's house, in my father's house
Joy and peace over there in my Father's house
There is peace, peace, peace

Walk With Me Lord, Walk With Me
Walk with me, Lord, walk with me
Walk with me, Lord, walk with me
All along this pilgrim journey
I want Jesus to walk with me

Be my guide, Lord, be my guide
Be my guide, Lord, be my guide
All along this pilgrim journey
I want Jesus to walk with me

I Will To Know
I will to know if He will welcome me there
I do not want to be denied
I want to meet Him in that city above
And with Him, I'll ever abide

They tell me of a home beyond the blue skies
A home where no dark clouds shall rise
Oh they tell me of a home in the skies
And with Him, I'll ever abide

I Love Jesus

I love Jesus (So do I)
I love Jesus (So do I)
I love Jesus (So do I)
I love Jesus (So do I)
I love Jesus (So do I)
I love Jesus He's my Savior
And He smiles and He loves me too

Glory Hallelujah (Praise the Lord)
Glory Hallelujah (Praise the Lord)
Glory Hallelujah (Praise the Lord)
Glory Hallelujah (Praise the Lord)
I love Jesus He's my Savior
And He smiles and He loves me too

Come By Here Good Lord, Come By Here

Come by here good Lord come by here
Come by here good Lord come by here
Come by here good Lord come by here
Oh Lord come by here

Somebody needs you Lord, come by here
Somebody needs you Lord, come by here
Somebody needs you Lord, come by here
Oh Lord, come by here

There Is Something Mighty Sweet About the Lord

There is something mighty sweet about the Lord
There is something mighty sweet about the Lord
Oh eyes haven't seen it and the ears haven't heard it
There is something mighty sweet about the Lord

I'm So Glad Jesus Lifted Me
I'm so glad, Jesus lifted me
I'm so glad, Jesus lifted me
I'm so glad, Jesus lifted me
Glory, Hallelujah, Jesus lifted me

Satan had me bound, but Jesus lifted me
Satan had me bound, but Jesus lifted me
Satan had me bound, but Jesus lifted me
Glory, Hallelujah, Jesus lifted me

I'm Pressing On, On All I Know

I'm pressing on, on all I know
I'm pressing on, everywhere I go
I'm pressing on, to that city
Where the mansions are prepared for me

Oh the press is on everywhere I go
I have some faith, but I'm asking for more
I'm pressing on, to that city
Where the mansions are prepared for me

If I Were You, I'd Make a Change

If I were you, I'd make a change
If I were you, I'd make a change
If I were you, I'd make a change
Oh my friends, don't you hear God calling,
"Make a change"

Backsliding girl, why don't you make a change
Backsliding girl, why don't you make a change
Backsliding girl, why don't you make a change
Oh my friends, don't you hear God calling,
"Make a change"

It Is Truly Wonderful

He pardoned my transgressions
He sanctified my soul
He honors my confessions
Since by His blood I'm whole

It is truly wonderful
What the Lord has done!
It is truly wonderful! (3x repeat)
What the Lord has done
Glory to His Name

He keeps me every moment
By trusting in His grace
'Tis through His blest atonement
That I may see His face
He brings me through affliction,
He leaves me not alone
He's with me in temptation
He keeps me for His own

He prospers and protects me
His blessings ever flow
He fills me with His glory
He makes me white as snow

He keeps me firm and faithful
His love I do enjoy
For this I shall be grateful
And live in His employ
There's not a single blessing
Which we receive on earth
That does not come from heaven
The source of our new birth

Words: Barney E. Warren, 1897

RESPONSIVE READINGS

Genesis 1:1-5, 26-28, 2:4, 7
In the beginning God created the heaven and the earth.

And the earth was without form, and void; and darkness was upon the face of the deep. And the Spirit of God moved upon the face of the waters.

And God said, Let there be light: and there was light.

And God saw the light, that it was good: and God divided the light from the darkness.

And God called the light Day, and the darkness he called Night. And the evening and the morning were the first day.

And God said, Let us make man in our image, after our likeness: and let them have dominion over the fish of the sea, and over the fowl of the air, and over the cattle, and over all the earth, and over every creeping thing that creepeth upon the earth.

So God created man in his own image, in the image of God created he him; male and female created he them.

And God blessed them, and God said unto them, Be fruitful, and multiply, and replenish the earth, and subdue it: and have dominion over the fish of the sea, and over the fowl of the air, and over every living thing that moveth upon the earth.

These are the generations of the heavens and of the earth when they were created, in the day that the Lord God made the earth and the heavens;

And the Lord God formed man of the dust of the ground, and breathed into his nostrils the breath of life; and man became a living soul.

Exodus 3: 7, 9-14
And the LORD said, I have surely seen the affliction of my people which are in Egypt, and have heard their cry by reason of their taskmasters; for I know their sorrows;

Now therefore, behold, the cry of the children of Israel is come unto me: and I have also seen the oppression wherewith the Egyptians oppress them.

Come now therefore, and I will send thee unto Pharaoh, that thou mayest bring forth my people the children of Israel out of Egypt.

And Moses said unto God, Who am I, that I should go unto Pharaoh, and that I should bring forth the children of Israel out of Egypt?

And he said, Certainly I will be with thee; and this shall be a token unto thee, that I have sent thee: When thou hast brought forth the people out of Egypt, ye shall serve God upon this mountain.

And Moses said unto God, Behold, when I come unto the children of Israel, and shall say unto them, The God of your fathers hath sent me unto you; and they shall say to me, What is his name? what shall I say unto them?

And God said unto Moses, I AM THAT I AM: and he said, Thus shalt thou say unto the children of Israel, I AM hath sent me unto you.

Deuteronomy 28: 1-6
And it shall come to pass, if thou shalt hearken diligently unto the voice of the LORD thy God, to observe and to do all his commandments which I command thee this day, that the LORD thy God will set thee on high above all nations of the earth:

And all these blessings shall come on thee, and overtake thee, if thou shalt hearken unto the voice of the LORD thy God.

Blessed shalt thou be in the city, and blessed shalt thou be in the field.

Blessed shall be the fruit of thy body, and the fruit of thy ground, and the fruit of thy cattle, the increase of thy kine, and the flocks of thy sheep.

Blessed shall be thy basket and thy store.

Blessed shalt thou be when thou comest in, and blessed shalt thou be when thou goest out.

Psalm 1:1-6

Blessed is the man that walketh not in the counsel of the ungodly, nor standeth in the way of sinners, nor sitteth in the seat of the scornful.

But his delight is in the law of the LORD; and in his law doth he meditate day and night.

And he shall be like a tree planted by the rivers of water, that bringeth forth his fruit in his season; his leaf also shall not wither; and whatsoever he doeth shall prosper.

The ungodly are not so: but are like the chaff which the wind driveth away.

Therefore the ungodly shall not stand in the judgment, nor sinners in the congregation of the righteous.

For the LORD knoweth the way of the righteous: but the way of the ungodly shall perish.

Psalm 8:1-9
O LORD, our Lord, how excellent is thy name in all the earth! who hast set thy glory above the heavens.

Out of the mouth of babes and sucklings hast thou ordained strength because of thine enemies, that thou mightest still the enemy and the avenger.

When I consider thy heavens, the work of thy fingers, the moon and the stars, which thou hast ordained;

What is man, that thou art mindful of him? and the son of man, that thou visitest him?

For thou hast made him a little lower than the angels, and hast crowned him with glory and honour.

Thou madest him to have dominion over the works of thy hands; thou hast put all things under his feet:

All sheep and oxen, yea, and the beasts of the field;

The fowl of the air, and the fish of the sea, and whatsoever passeth through the paths of the seas.

O LORD our Lord, how excellent is thy name in all the earth!

Psalm 23:1-6
The LORD is my shepherd; I shall not want.

He maketh me to lie down in green pastures: he leadeth me beside the still waters.

He restoreth my soul: he leadeth me in the paths of righteousness for his name's sake.

Yea, though I walk through the valley of the shadow of death, I will fear no evil: for thou art with me; thy rod and thy staff they comfort me.

Thou preparest a table before me in the presence of mine enemies: thou anointest my head with oil; my cup runneth over.

Surely goodness and mercy shall follow me all the days of my life: and I will dwell in the house of the LORD forever.

Psalm 24:1-10
The earth is the LORD's, and the fulness thereof; the world, and they that dwell therein.

For he hath founded it upon the seas, and established it upon the floods.

Who shall ascend into the hill of the LORD? or who shall stand in his holy place?

He that hath clean hands, and a pure heart; who hath not lifted up his soul unto vanity, nor sworn deceitfully.

He shall receive the blessing from the LORD, and righteousness from the God of his salvation.

This is the generation of them that seek him, that seek thy face, O Jacob. Selah.

Lift up your heads, O ye gates; and be ye lift up, ye everlasting doors; and the King of glory shall come in.

Who is this King of glory? The LORD strong and mighty, the LORD mighty in battle.

Lift up your heads, O ye gates; even lift them up, ye everlasting doors; and the King of glory shall come in.

Who is this King of glory? The LORD of hosts, he is the King of glory. Selah.

Psalm 27:1-14

The LORD is my light and my salvation; whom shall I fear? the LORD is the strength of my life; of whom shall I be afraid?

When the wicked, even mine enemies and my foes, came upon me to eat up my flesh, they stumbled and fell.

Though an host should encamp against me, my heart shall not fear: though war should rise against me, in this will I be confident.

One thing have I desired of the LORD, that will I seek after; that I may dwell in the house of the LORD all the days of my life, to behold the beauty of the LORD, and to enquire in his temple.

For in the time of trouble he shall hide me in his pavilion: in the secret of his tabernacle shall he hide me; he shall set me up upon a rock.

And now shall mine head be lifted up above mine enemies round about me: therefore will I offer in his tabernacle sacrifices of joy; I will sing, yea, I will sing praises unto the LORD.

Hear, O LORD, when I cry with my voice: have mercy also upon me, and answer me.

When thou saidst, Seek ye my face; my heart said unto thee, Thy face, LORD, will I seek.

Hide not thy face far from me; put not thy servant away in anger: thou hast been my help; leave me not, neither forsake me, O God of my salvation.

When my father and my mother forsake me, then the LORD will take me up.

Teach me thy way, O LORD, and lead me in a plain path, because of mine enemies.

Deliver me not over unto the will of mine enemies: for false witnesses are risen up against me, and such as breathe out cruelty.

I had fainted, unless I had believed to see the goodness of the LORD in the land of the living.

Wait on the LORD: be of good courage, and he shall strengthen thine heart: wait, I say, on the LORD.

Psalm 34:1-22

I will bless the LORD at all times: his praise shall continually be in my mouth.

My soul shall make her boast in the LORD: the humble shall hear thereof, and be glad.

O magnify the LORD with me, and let us exalt his name together.
I sought the LORD, and he heard me, and delivered me from all my fears.

They looked unto him, and were lightened: and their faces were not ashamed.

This poor man cried, and the LORD heard him, and saved him out of all his troubles.

The angel of the LORD encampeth round about them that fear him, and delivereth them.

O taste and see that the LORD is good: blessed is the man that trusteth in him.

O fear the LORD, ye his saints: for there is no want to them that fear him.

The young lions do lack, and suffer hunger: but they that seek the LORD shall not want any good thing.

Come, ye children, hearken unto me: I will teach you the fear of the LORD.

What man is he that desireth life, and loveth many days, that he may see good?

Keep thy tongue from evil, and thy lips from speaking guile.

Depart from evil, and do good; seek peace, and pursue it.

The eyes of the LORD are upon the righteous, and his ears are open unto their cry.

The face of the LORD is against them that do evil, to cut off the remembrance of them from the earth.

The righteous cry, and the LORD heareth, and delivereth them out of all their troubles.

The LORD is nigh unto them that are of a broken heart; and saveth such as be of a contrite spirit.

Many are the afflictions of the righteous: but the LORD delivereth him out of them all.

He keepeth all his bones: not one of them is broken.

Evil shall slay the wicked: and they that hate the righteous shall be desolate.

The LORD redeemeth the soul of his servants: and none of them that trust in him shall be desolate.

Psalm 40:1-17

I waited patiently for the Lord; and he inclined unto me, and heard my cry.

He brought me up also out of an horrible pit, out of the miry clay, and set my feet upon a rock, and established my goings.

And he hath put a new song in my mouth, even praise unto our God: many shall see it, and fear, and shall trust in the Lord.

Blessed is that man that maketh the Lord his trust, and respecteth not the proud, nor such as turn aside to lies.

Many, O Lord my God, are thy wonderful works which thou hast done, and thy thoughts which are to us-ward: they cannot be reckoned up in order unto thee: if I would declare and speak of them, they are more than can be numbered.

Sacrifice and offering thou didst not desire; mine ears hast thou opened: burnt offering and sin offering hast thou not required.

Then said I, Lo, I come: in the volume of the book it is written of me,

I delight to do thy will, O my God: yea, thy law is within my heart.

I have preached righteousness in the great congregation: lo, I have not refrained my lips, O Lord, thou knowest.

I have not hid thy righteousness within my heart; I have declared thy faithfulness and thy salvation: I have not concealed thy lovingkindness and thy truth from the great congregation.

Withhold not thou thy tender mercies from me, O Lord: let thy lovingkindness and thy truth continually preserve me.

For innumerable evils have compassed me about: mine iniquities have taken hold upon me, so that I am not able to look up; they are more than the hairs of mine head: therefore my heart faileth me.

Be pleased, O Lord, to deliver me: O Lord, make haste to help me.

Let them be ashamed and confounded together that seek after my soul to destroy it; let them be driven backward and put to shame that wish me evil.

Let them be desolate for a reward of their shame that say unto me, Aha, aha.

Let all those that seek thee rejoice and be glad in thee: let such as love thy salvation say continually, The Lord be magnified.

But I am poor and needy; yet the Lord thinketh upon me: thou art my help and my deliverer; make no tarrying, O my God.

Psalm 51:1-19
Have mercy upon me, O God, according to thy lovingkindness: according unto the multitude of thy tender mercies blot out my transgressions.

Wash me throughly from mine iniquity, and cleanse me from my sin.

For I acknowledge my transgressions: and my sin is ever before me.

Against thee, thee only, have I sinned, and done this evil in thy sight: that thou mightest be justified when thou speakest, and be clear when thou judgest.

Behold, I was shapen in iniquity; and in sin did my mother conceive me.

Behold, thou desirest truth in the inward parts: and in the hidden part thou shalt make me to know wisdom.

Purge me with hyssop, and I shall be clean: wash me, and I shall be whiter than snow.

Make me to hear joy and gladness; that the bones which thou hast broken may rejoice.

Hide thy face from my sins, and blot out all mine iniquities.

Create in me a clean heart, O God; and renew a right spirit within me.

Cast me not away from thy presence; and take not thy holy spirit from me.

Restore unto me the joy of thy salvation; and uphold me with thy free spirit.

Then will I teach transgressors thy ways; and sinners shall be converted unto thee.

Deliver me from blood guiltiness, O God, thou God of my salvation: and my tongue shall sing aloud of thy righteousness.

O Lord, open thou my lips; and my mouth shall shew forth thy praise.

For thou desirest not sacrifice; else would I give it: thou delightest not in burnt offering.

The sacrifices of God are a broken spirit: a broken and a contrite heart, O God, thou wilt not despise.

Do good in thy good pleasure unto Zion: build thou the walls of Jerusalem.

Then shalt thou be pleased with the sacrifices of righteousness, with burnt offering and whole burnt offering: then shall they offer bullocks upon thine altar.

Psalm 63:1-11
O God, thou art my God; early will I seek thee: my soul thirsteth for thee, my flesh longeth for thee in a dry and thirsty land, where no water is;

To see thy power and thy glory, so as I have seen thee in the sanctuary.

Because thy lovingkindness is better than life, my lips shall praise thee.

Thus will I bless thee while I live: I will lift up my hands in thy name.

My soul shall be satisfied as with marrow and fatness; and my mouth shall praise thee with joyful lips:

When I remember thee upon my bed, and meditate on thee in the night watches.

Because thou hast been my help, therefore in the shadow of thy wings will I rejoice.

My soul followeth hard after thee: thy right hand upholdeth me.

But those that seek my soul, to destroy it, shall go into the lower parts of the earth.

They shall fall by the sword: they shall be a portion for foxes.

But the king shall rejoice in God; every one that sweareth by him shall glory: but the mouth of them that speak lies shall be stopped.

Psalm 91:1-16

He that dwelleth in the secret place of the most High shall abide under the shadow of the Almighty.

I will say of the LORD, He is my refuge and my fortress: my God; in him will I trust.

Surely he shall deliver thee from the snare of the fowler, and from the noisome pestilence.

He shall cover thee with his feathers, and under his wings shalt thou trust: his truth shall be thy shield and buckler.

Thou shalt not be afraid for the terror by night; nor for the arrow that flieth by day;

Nor for the pestilence that walketh in darkness; nor for the destruction that wasteth at noonday.

A thousand shall fall at thy side, and ten thousand at thy right hand; but it shall not come nigh thee.

Only with thine eyes shalt thou behold and see the reward of the wicked.

Because thou hast made the LORD, which is my refuge, even the most High, thy habitation;

There shall no evil befall thee, neither shall any plague come nigh thy dwelling.

For he shall give his angels charge over thee, to keep thee in all thy ways.

They shall bear thee up in their hands, lest thou dash thy foot against a stone.

Thou shalt tread upon the lion and adder: the young lion and the dragon shalt thou trample under feet.

Because he hath set his love upon me, therefore will I deliver him: I will set him on high, because he hath known my name.

He shall call upon me, and I will answer him: I will be with him in trouble; I will deliver him, and honour him.

With long life will I satisfy him, and shew him my salvation.

Psalm 92:1-15
It is a good thing to give thanks unto the Lord, and to sing praises unto thy name, O Most High:

To shew forth thy lovingkindness in the morning, and thy faithfulness every night,

Upon an instrument of ten strings, and upon the psaltery; upon the harp with a solemn sound.

For thou, Lord, hast made me glad through thy work: I will triumph in the works of thy hands.

O Lord, how great are thy works! and thy thoughts are very deep.

A brutish man knoweth not; neither doth a fool understand this.

When the wicked spring as the grass, and when all the workers of iniquity do flourish; it is that they shall be destroyed forever:

But thou, Lord, art most high for evermore.

For, lo, thine enemies, O Lord, for, lo, thine enemies shall perish; all the workers of iniquity shall be scattered.

But my horn shalt thou exalt like the horn of an unicorn: I shall be anointed with fresh oil.

Mine eye also shall see my desire on mine enemies, and mine ears shall hear my desire of the wicked that rise up against me.

The righteous shall flourish like the palm tree: he shall grow like a cedar in Lebanon.

Those that be planted in the house of the Lord shall flourish in the courts of our God.

They shall still bring forth fruit in old age; they shall be fat and flourishing;

To shew that the Lord is upright: he is my rock, and there is no unrighteousness in him.

Psalm 93:1-5
The Lord reigneth, he is clothed with majesty; the Lord is clothed with strength, wherewith he hath girded himself: the world also is stablished, that it cannot be moved.

Thy throne is established of old: thou art from everlasting.

The floods have lifted up, O Lord, the floods have lifted up their voice; the floods lift up their waves.

The Lord on high is mightier than the noise of many waters, yea, than the mighty waves of the sea.

Thy testimonies are very sure: holiness becometh thine house, O Lord, forever.

Psalm 96:1-13
O sing unto the LORD a new song: sing unto the LORD, all the earth.

Sing unto the LORD, bless his name; shew forth his salvation from day to day.

Declare his glory among the heathen, his wonders among all people.

For the LORD is great, and greatly to be praised: he is to be feared above all gods.

For all the gods of the nations are idols: but the LORD made the heavens.

Honour and majesty are before him: strength and beauty are in his sanctuary.

Give unto the LORD, O ye kindreds of the people, give unto the LORD glory and strength.

Give unto the LORD the glory due unto his name: bring an offering, and come into his courts.

O worship the LORD in the beauty of holiness: fear before him, all the earth.

Say among the heathen that the LORD reigneth: the world also shall be established that it shall not be moved: he shall judge the people righteously.

Let the heavens rejoice, and let the earth be glad; let the sea roar, and the fulness thereof.

Let the field be joyful, and all that is therein: then shall all the trees of the wood rejoice

Before the LORD: for he cometh, for he cometh to judge the earth: he shall judge the world with righteousness, and the people with his truth.

Psalm 98:1-9
O sing unto the Lord a new song; for he hath done marvelous things: his right hand, and his holy arm, hath gotten him the victory.

The Lord hath made known his salvation: his righteousness hath he openly shewed in the sight of the heathen.

He hath remembered his mercy and his truth toward the house of Israel: all the ends of the earth have seen the salvation of our God.

Make a joyful noise unto the Lord, all the earth: make a loud noise, and rejoice, and sing praise.

Sing unto the Lord with the harp; with the harp, and the voice of a psalm.

With trumpets and sound of cornet make a joyful noise before the Lord, the King.

Let the sea roar, and the fulness thereof; the world, and they that dwell therein.

Let the floods clap their hands: let the hills be joyful together

Before the Lord; for he cometh to judge the earth: with righteousness shall he judge the world, and the people with equity.

Psalm 100:1-5
Make a joyful noise unto the LORD, all ye lands.

Serve the LORD with gladness: come before his presence with singing.

Know ye that the LORD he is God: it is he that hath made us, and not we ourselves; we are his people, and the sheep of his pasture.

Enter into his gates with thanksgiving, and into his courts with praise: be thankful unto him, and bless his name.

For the LORD is good; his mercy is everlasting; and his truth endureth to all generations.

Psalm 103:1-22

Bless the LORD, O my soul: and all that is within me, bless his holy name.

Bless the LORD, O my soul, and forget not all his benefits:

Who forgiveth all thine iniquities; who healeth all thy diseases;

Who redeemeth thy life from destruction; who crowneth thee with lovingkindness and tender mercies;

Who satisfieth thy mouth with good things; so that thy youth is renewed like the eagle's.

The LORD executeth righteousness and judgment for all that are oppressed.

He made known his ways unto Moses, his acts unto the children of Israel.

The LORD is merciful and gracious, slow to anger, and plenteous in mercy.

He will not always chide: neither will he keep his anger forever.

He hath not dealt with us after our sins; nor rewarded us according to our iniquities.

For as the heaven is high above the earth, so great is his mercy toward them that fear him.

As far as the east is from the west, so far hath he removed our transgressions from us.

Like as a father pitieth his children, so the LORD pitieth them that fear him.

For he knoweth our frame; he remembereth that we are dust.

As for man, his days are as grass: as a flower of the field, so he flourisheth.

For the wind passeth over it, and it is gone; and the place thereof shall know it no more.

But the mercy of the LORD is from everlasting to everlasting upon them that fear him, and his righteousness unto children's children;

To such as keep his covenant, and to those that remember his commandments to do them.

The LORD hath prepared his throne in the heavens; and his kingdom ruleth over all.

Bless the LORD, ye his angels, that excel in strength, that do his commandments, hearkening unto the voice of his word.

Bless ye the LORD, all ye his hosts; ye ministers of his, that do his pleasure.

Bless the LORD, all his works in all places of his dominion: bless the LORD, O my soul.

Psalm 121:1-8
I will lift up mine eyes unto the hills, from whence cometh my help.

My help cometh from the LORD, which made heaven and earth.

He will not suffer thy foot to be moved: he that keepeth thee will not slumber.

Behold, he that keepeth Israel shall neither slumber nor sleep.

The LORD is thy keeper: the LORD is thy shade upon thy right hand.

The sun shall not smite thee by day, nor the moon by night.

The LORD shall preserve thee from all evil: he shall preserve thy soul.

The LORD shall preserve thy going out and thy coming in from this time forth, and even for evermore.

Psalm 136: 1-26
O give thanks unto the Lord; for he is good: for his mercy endureth forever.

O give thanks unto the God of gods: for his mercy endureth forever.

O give thanks to the Lord of lords: for his mercy endureth forever.

To him who alone doeth great wonders: for his mercy endureth forever.

To him that by wisdom made the heavens: for his mercy endureth forever.

To him that stretched out the earth above the waters: for his mercy endureth forever.

To him that made great lights: for his mercy endureth forever:

The sun to rule by day: for his mercy endureth forever:

The moon and stars to rule by night: for his mercy endureth forever.

To him that smote Egypt in their firstborn: for his mercy endureth forever:

And brought out Israel from among them: for his mercy endureth forever:

With a strong hand, and with a stretched out arm: for his mercy endureth forever.

To him which divided the Red sea into parts: for his mercy endureth forever:
And made Israel to pass through the midst of it: for his mercy endureth forever:

But overthrew Pharaoh and his host in the Red sea: for his mercy endureth forever.

To him which led his people through the wilderness: for his mercy endureth forever.

To him which smote great kings: for his mercy endureth forever:

And slew famous kings: for his mercy endureth forever:

Sihon king of the Amorites: for his mercy endureth for ever:
And Og the king of Bashan: for his mercy endureth forever:

And gave their land for an heritage: for his mercy endureth forever:

Even an heritage unto Israel his servant: for his mercy endureth forever.

Who remembered us in our low estate: for his mercy endureth forever:

And hath redeemed us from our enemies: for his mercy endureth forever.

Who giveth food to all flesh: for his mercy endureth forever.

O give thanks unto the God of heaven: for his mercy endureth forever.

Psalm 139:1-24
O lord, thou hast searched me, and known me.

Thou knowest my downsitting and mine uprising, thou understandest my thought afar off.

Thou compassest my path and my lying down, and art acquainted with all my ways.

For there is not a word in my tongue, but, lo, O Lord, thou knowest it altogether.

Thou hast beset me behind and before, and laid thine hand upon me.

Such knowledge is too wonderful for me; it is high, I cannot attain unto it.

Whither shall I go from thy spirit? or whither shall I flee from thy presence?

If I ascend up into heaven, thou art there: if I make my bed in hell, behold, thou art there.

If I take the wings of the morning, and dwell in the uttermost parts of the sea;

Even there shall thy hand lead me, and thy right hand shall hold me.

If I say, Surely the darkness shall cover me; even the night shall be light about me.

Yea, the darkness hideth not from thee; but the night shineth as the day: the darkness and the light are both alike to thee.

For thou hast possessed my reins: thou hast covered me in my mother's womb.

I will praise thee; for I am fearfully and wonderfully made: marvellous are thy works; and that my soul knoweth right well.

My substance was not hid from thee, when I was made in secret, and curiously wrought in the lowest parts of the earth.

Thine eyes did see my substance, yet being unperfect; and in thy book all my members were written, which in continuance were fashioned, when as yet there was none of them.

How precious also are thy thoughts unto me, O God! how great is the sum of them!

If I should count them, they are more in number than the sand: when I awake, I am still with thee.

Surely thou wilt slay the wicked, O God: depart from me therefore, ye bloody men.

For they speak against thee wickedly, and thine enemies take thy name in vain.

Do not I hate them, O Lord, that hate thee? and am not I grieved with those that rise up against thee?

I hate them with perfect hatred: I count them mine enemies.

Search me, O God, and know my heart: try me, and know my thoughts:

And see if there be any wicked way in me, and lead me in the way everlasting.

Psalm 145:1-21
I will extol thee, my God, O king; and I will bless thy name for ever and ever.

Every day will I bless thee; and I will praise thy name for ever and ever.

Great is the Lord, and greatly to be praised; and his greatness is unsearchable.

One generation shall praise thy works to another, and shall declare thy mighty acts.

I will speak of the glorious honour of thy majesty, and of thy wondrous works.

And men shall speak of the might of thy terrible acts: and I will declare thy greatness.

They shall abundantly utter the memory of thy great goodness and shall sing of thy righteousness.

The Lord is gracious, and full of compassion; slow to anger, and of great mercy.

The Lord is good to all: and his tender mercies are over all his works.

All thy works shall praise thee, O Lord; and thy saints shall bless thee.

They shall speak of the glory of thy kingdom, and talk of thy power;

To make known to the sons of men his mighty acts, and the glorious majesty of his kingdom.

Thy kingdom is an everlasting kingdom, and thy dominion endureth throughout all generations.

The Lord upholdeth all that fall, and raiseth up all those that be bowed down.

The eyes of all wait upon thee; and thou givest them their meat in due season.

Thou openest thine hand, and satisfiest the desire of every living thing.

The Lord is righteous in all his ways, and holy in all his works.

The Lord is nigh unto all them that call upon him, to all that call upon him in truth.

He will fulfil the desire of them that fear him: he also will hear their cry, and will save them.

The Lord preserveth all them that love him: but all the wicked will he destroy.

My mouth shall speak the praise of the Lord: and let all flesh bless his holy name for ever and ever.

Psalm 150:1-6

Praise ye the LORD. Praise God in his sanctuary: praise him in the firmament of his power.

Praise him for his mighty acts: praise him according to his excellent greatness.

Praise him with the sound of the trumpet: praise him with the psaltery and harp.

Praise him with the timbrel and dance: praise him with stringed instruments and organs.

Praise him upon the loud cymbals: praise him upon the high sounding cymbals.

Let everything that hath breath praise the LORD. Praise ye the LORD.

Proverbs 3:1-12
My son, forget not my law; but let thine heart keep my commandments:

For length of days, and long life, and peace, shall they add to thee.

Let not mercy and truth forsake thee: bind them about thy neck; write them upon the table of thine heart:

So shalt thou find favour and good understanding in the sight of God and man.

Trust in the LORD with all thine heart; and lean not unto thine own understanding.

In all thy ways acknowledge him, and he shall direct thy paths.

Be not wise in thine own eyes: fear the LORD, and depart from evil.

It shall be health to thy navel, and marrow to thy bones.

Honour the LORD with thy substance, and with the firstfruits of all thine increase:

So shall thy barns be filled with plenty, and thy presses shall burst out with new wine.

My son, despise not the chastening of the LORD; neither be weary of his correction:

For whom the LORD loveth he correcteth; even as a father the son in whom he delighteth.

Proverbs 31:10-31
Who can find a virtuous woman? for her price is far above rubies.

The heart of her husband doth safely trust in her, so that he shall have no need of spoil.

She will do him good and not evil all the days of her life.

She seeketh wool, and flax, and worketh willingly with her hands.

She is like the merchants' ships; she bringeth her food from afar.

She riseth also while it is yet night, and giveth meat to her household, and a portion to her maidens.

She considereth a field, and buyeth it: with the fruit of her hands she planteth a vineyard.

She girdeth her loins with strength, and strengtheneth her arms.

She perceiveth that her merchandise is good: her candle goeth not out by night.

She layeth her hands to the spindle, and her hands hold the distaff.

She stretcheth out her hand to the poor; yea, she reacheth forth her hands to the needy.

She is not afraid of the snow for her household: for all her household are clothed with scarlet.

She maketh herself coverings of tapestry; her clothing is silk and purple.

Her husband is known in the gates, when he sitteth among the elders of the land.

She maketh fine linen, and selleth it; and delivereth girdles unto the merchant.

Strength and honour are her clothing; and she shall rejoice in time to come.

She openeth her mouth with wisdom; and in her tongue is the law of kindness.

She looketh well to the ways of her household, and eateth not the bread of idleness.

Her children arise up, and call her blessed; her husband also, and he praiseth her.

Many daughters have done virtuously, but thou excellest them all.

Favour is deceitful, and beauty is vain: but a woman that feareth the LORD, she shall be praised.

Give her of the fruit of her hands; and let her own works praise her in the gates.

Ecclesiastes 3:1-8

To everything there is a season, and a time to every purpose under the heaven:

A time to be born, and a time to die; a time to plant, and a time to pluck up that which is planted;

A time to kill, and a time to heal; a time to break down, and a time to build up;

A time to weep, and a time to laugh; a time to mourn, and a time to dance;

A time to cast away stones, and a time to gather stones together; a time to embrace, and a time to refrain from embracing;

A time to get, and a time to lose; a time to keep, and a time to cast away;

A time to rend, and a time to sew; a time to keep silence, and a time to speak;

A time to love, and a time to hate; a time of war, and a time of peace.

Isaiah 53:1-5

Who hath believed our report? and to whom is the arm of the LORD revealed?

For he shall grow up before him as a tender plant, and as a root out of a dry ground: he hath no form nor comeliness; and when we shall see him, there is no beauty that we should desire him.

He is despised and rejected of men; a man of sorrows, and acquainted with grief: and we hid as it were our faces from him; he was despised, and we esteemed him not.

Surely he hath borne our griefs, and carried our sorrows: yet we did esteem him stricken, smitten of God, and afflicted.

But he was wounded for our transgressions, he was bruised for our iniquities: the chastisement of our peace was upon him; and with his stripes we are healed.

All we like sheep have gone astray; we have turned every one to his own way; and the LORD hath laid on him the iniquity of us all.

He was oppressed, and he was afflicted, yet he opened not his mouth: he is brought as a lamb to the slaughter, and as a sheep before her shearers is dumb, so he openeth not his mouth.

He was taken from prison and from judgment: and who shall declare his generation? for he was cut off out of the land of the living: for the transgression of my people was he stricken.

And he made his grave with the wicked, and with the rich in his death; because he had done no violence, neither was any deceit in his mouth.

Yet it pleased the LORD to bruise him; he hath put him to grief: when thou shalt make his soul an offering for sin, he shall see his seed, he shall prolong his days, and the pleasure of the LORD shall prosper in his hand.

He shall see of the travail of his soul, and shall be satisfied: by his knowledge shall my righteous servant justify many; for he shall bear their iniquities.

Therefore will I divide him a portion with the great, and he shall divide the spoil with the strong; because he hath poured out his soul unto death: and he was numbered with the transgressors; and he bare the sin of many, and made intercession for the transgressors.

Matthew 1:18-23
Now the birth of Jesus Christ was on this wise: When as his mother Mary was espoused to Joseph, before they came together, she was found with child of the Holy Ghost.

Then Joseph her husband, being a just man, and not willing to make her a public example, was minded to put her away privily.

But while he thought on these things, behold, the angel of the LORD appeared unto him in a dream, saying, Joseph, thou son of David, fear not to take unto thee Mary thy wife: for that which is conceived in her is of the Holy Ghost.

And she shall bring forth a son, and thou shalt call his name JESUS: for he shall save his people from their sins.

Now all this was done, that it might be fulfilled which was spoken of the Lord by the prophet, saying,

Behold, a virgin shall be with child, and shall bring forth a son, and they shall call his name Emmanuel, which being interpreted is, God with us.

Matthew 5:3-12

Blessed are the poor in spirit: for theirs is the kingdom of heaven.

Blessed are they that mourn: for they shall be comforted.

Blessed are the meek: for they shall inherit the earth.

Blessed are they which do hunger and thirst after righteousness: for they shall be filled.

Blessed are the merciful: for they shall obtain mercy.

Blessed are the pure in heart: for they shall see God.

Blessed are the peacemakers: for they shall be called the children of God.

Blessed are they which are persecuted for righteousness' sake: for theirs is the kingdom of heaven.

Blessed are ye, when men shall revile you, and persecute you, and shall say all manner of evil against you falsely, for my sake.

Rejoice, and be exceeding glad: for great is your reward in heaven: for so persecuted they the prophets which were before you.

Matthew 28:1-10
In the end of the sabbath, as it began to dawn toward the first day of the week, came Mary Magdalene and the other Mary to see the sepulchre.

And, behold, there was a great earthquake: for the angel of the Lord descended from heaven, and came and rolled back the stone from the door, and sat upon it.

His countenance was like lightning, and his raiment white as snow:

And for fear of him the keepers did shake, and became as dead men.

And the angel answered and said unto the women, Fear not ye: for I know that ye seek Jesus, which was crucified.

He is not here: for he is risen, as he said. Come, see the place where the Lord lay.

And go quickly, and tell his disciples that he is risen from the dead; and, behold, he goeth before you into Galilee; there shall ye see him: lo, I have told you.

And they departed quickly from the sepulchre with fear and great joy; and did run to bring his disciples word.

And as they went to tell his disciples, behold, Jesus met them, saying, All hail. And they came and held him by the feet, and worshipped him.

Then said Jesus unto them, Be not afraid: go tell my brethren that they go into Galilee, and there shall they see me.

Mark 11:1-10

And when they came nigh to Jerusalem, unto Bethphage and Bethany, at the Mount of Olives, he sendeth forth two of his disciples,

And saith unto them, Go your way into the village over against you: and as soon as ye be entered into it, ye shall find a colt tied, whereon never man sat; loose him, and bring him.

And if any man say unto you, Why do ye this? say ye that the Lord hath need of him; and straightway he will send him hither.

And they went their way, and found the colt tied by the door without in a place where two ways met; and they loose him.

And certain of them that stood there said unto them, What do ye, loosing the colt?

And they said unto them even as Jesus had commanded: and they let them go.

And they brought the colt to Jesus, and cast their garments on him; and he sat upon him.
And many spread their garments in the way: and others cut down branches off the trees, and strawed them in the way.

And they that went before, and they that followed, cried, saying, Hosanna; Blessed is he that cometh in the name of the Lord:

Blessed be the kingdom of our father David, that cometh in the name of the Lord: Hosanna in the highest.

Mark 16:14-20

Afterward he appeared unto the eleven as they sat at meat and upbraided them with their unbelief and hardness of heart, because they believed not them which had seen him after he was risen.

And he said unto them, Go ye into all the world, and preach the gospel to every creature.

He that believeth and is baptized shall be saved; but he that believeth not shall be damned.

And these signs shall follow them that believe; In my name shall they cast out devils; they shall speak with new tongues;

They shall take up serpents; and if they drink any deadly thing, it shall not hurt them; they shall lay hands on the sick, and they shall recover.

So then after the Lord had spoken unto them, he was received up into heaven, and sat on the right hand of God.

Luke 2:1-14

And it came to pass in those days, that there went out a decree from Caesar Augustus that all the world should be taxed.

And this taxing was first made when Cyrenius was governor of Syria.

And all went to be taxed, every one into his own city.

And Joseph also went up from Galilee, out of the city of Nazareth, into Judaea, unto the city of David, which is called Bethlehem; because he was of the house and lineage of David:

To be taxed with Mary his espoused wife, being great with child.

And so it was, that, while they were there, the days were accomplished that she should be delivered.

And she brought forth her firstborn son, and wrapped him in swaddling clothes, and laid him in a manger; because there was no room for them in the inn.

And there were in the same country shepherds abiding in the field, keeping watch over their flock by night.

And, lo, the angel of the Lord came upon them, and the glory of the Lord shone round about them: and they were sore afraid.

And the angel said unto them, Fear not: for, behold, I bring you good tidings of great joy, which shall be to all people.

For unto you is born this day in the city of David a Savior, which is Christ the Lord.

And this shall be a sign unto you; Ye shall find the babe wrapped in swaddling clothes, lying in a manger.

And suddenly there was with the angel a multitude of the heavenly host praising God, and saying,

Glory to God in the highest, and on earth peace, good will toward men.

Luke 22:7-20

Then came the day of unleavened bread, when the Passover must be killed.

And he sent Peter and John, saying, Go and prepare us the Passover, that we may eat.

And they said unto him, Where wilt thou that we prepare?

And he said unto them, Behold, when ye are entered into the city, there shall a man meet you, bearing a pitcher of water; follow him into the house where he entereth in.

And ye shall say unto the good man of the house, The Master saith unto thee, Where is the guest chamber, where I shall eat the Passover with my disciples?

And he shall shew you a large upper room furnished: there make ready.

And they went, and found as he had said unto them: and they made ready the Passover.

And when the hour was come, he sat down, and the twelve apostles with him.

And he said unto them, With desire I have desired to eat this Passover with you before I suffer:

For I say unto you, I will not any more eat thereof, until it be fulfilled in the kingdom of God.

And he took the cup, and gave thanks, and said, Take this, and divide it among yourselves:

For I say unto you, I will not drink of the fruit of the vine, until the kingdom of God shall come.

And he took bread, and gave thanks, and brake it, and gave unto them, saying, This is my body which is given for you: this do in remembrance of me.

Likewise also the cup after supper, saying, This cup is the new testament in my blood, which is shed for you.

John 1:1-5, 10-14
In the beginning was the Word, and the Word was with God, and the Word was God.

The same was in the beginning with God.

All things were made by him; and without him was not anything made that was made.

In him was life; and the life was the light of men.

And the light shineth in darkness; and the darkness comprehended it not.

He was in the world, and the world was made by him, and the world knew him not.

He came unto his own, and his own received him not.

But as many as received him, to them gave he power to become the sons of God, even to them that believe on his name:

Which were born, not of blood, nor of the will of the flesh, nor of the will of man, but of God.

And the Word was made flesh, and dwelt among us, (and we beheld his glory, the glory as of the only begotten of the Father,) full of grace and truth.

John 14:1-14

Let not your heart be troubled: ye believe in God, believe also in me.

In my Father's house are many mansions: if it were not so, I would have told you. I go to prepare a place for you.

And if I go and prepare a place for you, I will come again, and receive you unto myself; that where I am, there ye may be also.

And whither I go ye know, and the way ye know.

Thomas saith unto him, Lord, we know not whither thou goest; and how can we know the way?

Jesus saith unto him, I am the way, the truth, and the life: no man cometh unto the Father, but by me.

If ye had known me, ye should have known my Father also: and from henceforth ye know him, and have seen him.

Philip saith unto him, Lord, show us the Father, and it sufficeth us.

Jesus saith unto him, Have I been so long time with you, and yet hast thou not known me, Philip? he that hath seen me hath seen the Father; and how sayest thou then, Show us the Father?

Believest thou not that I am in the Father, and the Father in me? the words that I speak unto you I speak not of myself: but the Father that dwelleth in me, he doeth the works.

Believe me that I am in the Father, and the Father in me: or else believe me for the very works' sake.

Verily, verily, I say unto you, He that believeth on me, the works that I do shall he do also; and greater works than these shall he do; because I go unto my Father.

And whatsoever ye shall ask in my name, that will I do, that the Father may be glorified in the Son.

If ye shall ask any thing in my name, I will do it.

John 15:1-7

I am the true vine, and my Father is the husbandman.

Every branch in me that beareth not fruit he taketh away: and every branch that beareth fruit, he purgeth it, that it may bring forth more fruit.

Now ye are clean through the word which I have spoken unto you.

Abide in me, and I in you. As the branch cannot bear fruit of itself, except it abide in the vine; no more can ye, except ye abide in me.

I am the vine, ye are the branches: He that abideth in me, and I in him, the same bringeth forth much fruit: for without me ye can do nothing.

If a man abide not in me, he is cast forth as a branch, and is withered; and men gather them, and cast them into the fire, and they are burned.

If ye abide in me, and my words abide in you, ye shall ask what ye will, and it shall be done unto you.

Acts 2:1-8, 12-18, 38-39
And when the day of Pentecost was fully come, they were all with one accord in one place.

And suddenly there came a sound from heaven as of a rushing mighty wind, and it filled all the house where they were sitting.

And there appeared unto them cloven tongues like as of fire, and it sat upon each of them.

And they were all filled with the Holy Ghost, and began to speak with other tongues, as the Spirit gave them utterance.

And there were dwelling at Jerusalem Jews, devout men, out of every nation under heaven.

Now when this was noised abroad, the multitude came together, and were confounded, because that every man heard them speak in his own language.

And they were all amazed and marvelled, saying one to another, Behold, are not all these which speak Galilaeans?

And how hear we every man in our own tongue, wherein we were born?

And they were all amazed, and were in doubt, saying one to another, What meaneth this?

Others mocking said, These men are full of new wine.

But Peter, standing up with the eleven, lifted up his voice, and said unto them, Ye men of Judaea, and all ye that dwell at Jerusalem, be this known unto you, and hearken to my words:

For these are not drunken, as ye suppose, seeing it is but the third hour of the day.

But this is that which was spoken by the prophet Joel;

And it shall come to pass in the last days, saith God, I will pour out of my Spirit upon all flesh: and your sons and your daughters shall prophesy, and your young men shall see visions, and your old men shall dream dreams:

And on my servants and on my handmaidens I will pour out in those days of my Spirit; and they shall prophesy:

Then Peter said unto them, Repent, and be baptized every one of you in the name of Jesus Christ for the remission of sins, and ye shall receive the gift of the Holy Ghost.

For the promise is unto you, and to your children, and to all that are afar off, even as many as the LORD our God shall call.

Romans 5:1-10
Therefore, being justified by faith, we have peace with God through our Lord Jesus Christ:

By whom also we have access by faith into this grace wherein we stand, and rejoice in hope of the glory of God.

And not only so, but we glory in tribulations also: knowing that tribulation worketh patience;

And patience, experience; and experience, hope:

And hope maketh not ashamed; because the love of God is shed abroad in our hearts by the Holy Ghost which is given unto us.

For when we were yet without strength, in due time Christ died for the ungodly.

For scarcely for a righteous man will one die: yet peradventure for a good man some would even dare to die.

But God commendeth his love toward us, in that, while we were yet sinners, Christ died for us.

Much more then, being now justified by his blood, we shall be saved from wrath through him.

For if, when we were enemies, we were reconciled to God by the death of his Son, much more, being reconciled, we shall be saved by his life.

Romans 8:1-15
There is therefore now no condemnation to them which are in Christ Jesus, who walk not after the flesh, but after the Spirit.

For the law of the Spirit of life in Christ Jesus hath made me free from the law of sin and death.

For what the law could not do, in that it was weak through the flesh, God sending his own Son in the likeness of sinful flesh, and for sin, condemned sin in the flesh:

That the righteousness of the law might be fulfilled in us, who walk not after the flesh, but after the Spirit.

For they that are after the flesh do mind the things of the flesh; but they that are after the Spirit the things of the Spirit.

For to be carnally minded is death; but to be spiritually minded is life and peace.

Because the carnal mind is enmity against God: for it is not subject to the law of God, neither indeed can be.

So then they that are in the flesh cannot please God.

But ye are not in the flesh, but in the Spirit, if so be that the Spirit of God dwell in you. Now if any man have not the Spirit of Christ, he is none of his.

And if Christ be in you, the body is dead because of sin; but the Spirit is life because of righteousness.

But if the Spirit of him that raised up Jesus from the dead dwell in you, he that raised up Christ from the dead shall also quicken your mortal bodies by his Spirit that dwelleth in you.

Therefore, brethren, we are debtors, not to the flesh, to live after the flesh.

For if ye live after the flesh, ye shall die: but if ye through the Spirit do mortify the deeds of the body, ye shall live.

For as many as are led by the Spirit of God, they are the sons of God.

For ye have not received the spirit of bondage again to fear; but ye have received the Spirit of adoption, whereby we cry, Abba, Father.

Romans 8:28-39
And we know that all things work together for good to them that love God, to them who are the called according to his purpose.

For whom he did foreknow, he also did predestinate to be conformed to the image of his Son, that he might be the firstborn among many brethren.

Moreover whom he did predestinate, them he also called: and whom he called, them he also justified: and whom he justified, them he also glorified.

What shall we then say to these things? If God be for us, who can be against us?

He that spared not his own Son, but delivered him up for us all, how shall he not with him also freely give us all things?

Who shall lay anything to the charge of God's elect? It is God that justifieth.

Who is he that condemneth? It is Christ that died, yea rather, that is risen again, who is even at the right hand of God, who also maketh intercession for us.

Who shall separate us from the love of Christ? shall tribulation, or distress, or persecution, or famine, or nakedness, or peril, or sword?

As it is written, For thy sake we are killed all the day long; we are accounted as sheep for the slaughter.

Nay, in all these things we are more than conquerors through him that loved us.

For I am persuaded, that neither death, nor life, nor angels, nor principalities, nor powers, nor things present, nor things to come,

Nor height, nor depth, nor any other creature, shall be able to separate us from the love of God, which is in Christ Jesus our Lord.

1 Corinthians 11:20-34

When ye come together therefore into one place, this is not to eat the Lord's supper.

For in eating every one taketh before other his own supper: and one is hungry, and another is drunken.

What? have ye not houses to eat and to drink in? or despise ye the church of God, and shame them that have not? what shall I say to you? shall I praise you in this? I praise you not.

For I have received of the Lord that which also I delivered unto you, that the Lord Jesus the same night in which he was betrayed took bread:

And when he had given thanks, he brake it, and said, Take, eat: this is my body, which is broken for you: this do in remembrance of me.

After the same manner also he took the cup, when he had supped, saying, this cup is the new testament in my blood: this do ye, as oft as ye drink it, in remembrance of me.

For as often as ye eat this bread, and drink this cup, ye do shew the Lord's death till he come.

Wherefore whosoever shall eat this bread, and drink this cup of the Lord, unworthily, shall be guilty of the body and blood of the Lord.

But let a man examine himself, and so let him eat of that bread, and drink of that cup.

For he that eateth and drinketh unworthily, eateth and drinketh damnation to himself, not discerning the Lord's body.

For this cause many are weak and sickly among you, and many sleep.

For if we would judge ourselves, we should not be judged.

But when we are judged, we are chastened of the Lord, that we should not be condemned with the world.

Wherefore, my brethren, when ye come together to eat, tarry one for another.

And if any man hunger, let him eat at home; that ye come not together unto condemnation. And the rest will I set in order when I come.

1 Corinthians 12:1-14
Now concerning spiritual gifts, brethren, I would not have you ignorant.

Ye know that ye were Gentiles, carried away unto these dumb idols, even as ye were led.

Wherefore I give you to understand, that no man speaking by the Spirit of God calleth Jesus accursed: and that no man can say that Jesus is the Lord, but by the Holy Ghost.

Now there are diversities of gifts, but the same Spirit.

And there are differences of administrations, but the same Lord.

And there are diversities of operations, but it is the same God which worketh all in all.

But the manifestation of the Spirit is given to every man to profit withal.
For to one is given by the Spirit the word of wisdom; to another the word of knowledge by the same Spirit;

To another faith by the same Spirit; to another the gifts of healing by the same Spirit;

To another the working of miracles; to another prophecy; to another discerning of spirits; to another divers kinds of tongues; to another the interpretation of tongues:

But all these worketh that one and the selfsame Spirit, dividing to every man severally as he will.

For as the body is one, and hath many members, and all the members of that one body, being many, are one body: so also is Christ.

For by one Spirit are we all baptized into one body, whether we be Jews or Gentiles, whether we be bond or free; and have been all made to drink into one Spirit.

For the body is not one member, but many.

1 Corinthians 13:1-10
Tough I speak with the tongues of men and of angels, and have not charity, I am become as sounding brass, or a tinkling cymbal.

And though I have the gift of prophecy, and understand all mysteries, and all knowledge; and though I have all faith, so that I could remove mountains, and have not charity, I am nothing.

And though I bestow all my goods to feed the poor, and though I give my body to be burned, and have not charity, it profiteth me nothing.

Charity suffereth long, and is kind; charity envieth not; charity vaunteth not itself, is not puffed up,

Doth not behave itself unseemly, seeketh not her own, is not easily provoked, thinketh no evil;

Rejoiceth not in iniquity, but rejoiceth in the truth;

Beareth all things, believeth all things, hopeth all things, endureth all things.

Charity never faileth: but whether there be prophecies, they shall fail; whether there be tongues, they shall cease; whether there be knowledge, it shall vanish away.

For we know in part, and we prophesy in part.

But when that which is perfect is come, then that which is in part shall be done away.

When I was a child, I spake as a child, I understood as a child, I thought as a child: but when I became a man, I put away childish things.

For now we see through a glass, darkly; but then face to face: now I know in part; but then shall I know even as also I am known.

And now abideth faith, hope, charity, these three; but the greatest of these is charity.

1 Corinthians 15:12-28, 50-58

Now if Christ be preached that he rose from the dead, how say some among you that there is no resurrection of the dead?

But if there be no resurrection of the dead, then is Christ not risen:

And if Christ be not risen, then is our preaching vain, and your faith is also vain.

Yea, and we are found false witnesses of God; because we have testified of God that he raised up Christ: whom he raised not up, if so be that the dead rise not.

For if the dead rise not, then is not Christ raised:

And if Christ be not raised, your faith is vain; ye are yet in your sins.

Then they also which are fallen asleep in Christ are perished.

If in this life only we have hope in Christ, we are of all men most miserable.

But now is Christ risen from the dead, and become the firstfruits of them that slept.

For since by man came death, by man came also the resurrection of the dead.

For as in Adam all die, even so in Christ shall all be made alive.

For he must reign, till he hath put all enemies under his feet.

The last enemy that shall be destroyed is death.

For he hath put all things under his feet. But when he saith all things are put under him, it is manifest that he is excepted, which did put all things under him.

And when all things shall be subdued unto him, then shall the Son also himself be subject unto him that put all things under him, that God may be all in all.

Now this I say, brethren, that flesh and blood cannot inherit the kingdom of God; neither doth corruption inherit incorruption.

Behold, I shew you a mystery; We shall not all sleep, but we shall all be changed,

In a moment, in the twinkling of an eye, at the last trump: for the trumpet shall sound, and the dead shall be raised incorruptible, and we shall be changed.

For this corruptible must put on incorruption, and this mortal must put on immortality.

So when this corruptible shall have put on incorruption, and this mortal shall have put on immortality, then shall be brought to pass the saying that is written, Death is swallowed up in victory.

O death, where is thy sting? O grave, where is thy victory?

The sting of death is sin; and the strength of sin is the law.

But thanks be to God, which giveth us the victory through our Lord Jesus Christ.

Therefore, my beloved brethren, be ye stedfast, unmoveable, always abounding in the work of the Lord,

forasmuch as ye know that your labour is not in vain in the Lord.

Ephesians 2:1-10
And you hath he quickened, who were dead in trespasses and sins;

Wherein in time past ye walked according to the course of this world, according to the prince of the power of the air, the spirit that now worketh in the children of disobedience:

Among whom also we all had our conversation in times past in the lusts of our flesh, fulfilling the desires of the flesh and of the mind; and were by nature the children of wrath, even as others.

But God, who is rich in mercy, for his great love wherewith he loved us,

Even when we were dead in sins, hath quickened us together with Christ, (by grace ye are saved;)

And hath raised us up together, and made us sit together in heavenly places in Christ Jesus:

That in the ages to come he might shew the exceeding riches of his grace in his kindness toward us through Christ Jesus.

For by grace are ye saved through faith; and that not of yourselves: it is the gift of God:

Not of works, lest any man should boast.

For we are his workmanship, created in Christ Jesus unto good works, which God hath before ordained that we should walk in them.

Ephesians 4:1-15
I therefore, the prisoner of the Lord, beseech you that ye walk worthy of the vocation wherewith ye are called,

With all lowliness and meekness, with longsuffering, forbearing one another in love;

Endeavouring to keep the unity of the Spirit in the bond of peace.

There is one body, and one Spirit, even as ye are called in one hope of your calling;

One Lord, one faith, one baptism,

One God and Father of all, who is above all, and through all, and in you all.

But unto every one of us is given grace according to the measure of the gift of Christ.

Wherefore he saith, When he ascended up on high, he led captivity captive, and gave gifts unto men.

(Now that he ascended, what is it but that he also descended first into the lower parts of the earth?

He that descended is the same also that ascended up far above all heavens, that he might fill all things.)

And he gave some, apostles; and some, prophets; and some, evangelists; and some, pastors and teachers;

For the perfecting of the saints, for the work of the ministry, for the edifying of the body of Christ:

Till we all come in the unity of the faith, and of the knowledge of the Son of God, unto a perfect man, unto the measure of the stature of the fulness of Christ:

That we henceforth be no more children, tossed to and fro, and carried about with every wind of doctrine, by the sleight of men, and cunning craftiness, whereby they lie in wait to deceive;

But speaking the truth in love, may grow up into him in all things, which is the head, even Christ:

Ephesians 6:10-18
Finally, my brethren, be strong in the Lord, and in the power of his might.

Put on the whole armour of God, that ye may be able to stand against the wiles of the devil.

For we wrestle not against flesh and blood, but against principalities, against powers, against the rulers of the darkness of this world, against spiritual wickedness in high places.

Wherefore take unto you the whole armour of God, that ye may be able to withstand in the evil day, and having done all, to stand.

Stand therefore, having your loins girt about with truth, and having on the breastplate of righteousness;

And your feet shod with the preparation of the gospel of peace;

Above all, taking the shield of faith, wherewith ye shall be able to quench all the fiery darts of the wicked.

And take the helmet of salvation, and the sword of the Spirit, which is the word of God:

Praying always with all prayer and supplication in the Spirit, and watching thereunto with all perseverance and supplication for all saints;

Philippians 2:1-11

If there be therefore any consolation in Christ, if any comfort of love, if any fellowship of the Spirit, if any bowels and mercies,

Fulfil ye my joy, that ye be likeminded, having the same love, being of one accord of one mind.

Let nothing be done through strife or vainglory; but in lowliness of mind let each esteem other better than themselves.

Look not every man on his own things, but every man also on the things of others.

Let this mind be in you, which was also in Christ Jesus:

Who, being in the form of God, thought it not robbery to be equal with God:

But made himself of no reputation, and took upon him the form of a servant, and was made in the likeness of men:

And being found in fashion as a man, he humbled himself, and became obedient unto death, even the death of the cross.

Wherefore God also hath highly exalted him, and given him a name which is above every name:

That at the name of Jesus every knee should bow, of things in heaven, and things in earth, and things under the earth;

And that every tongue should confess that Jesus Christ is Lord, to the glory of God the Father.

Colossians 1:12-20

Giving thanks unto the Father, which hath made us meet to be partakers of the inheritance of the saints in light:

Who hath delivered us from the power of darkness, and hath translated us into the kingdom of his dear Son:

In whom we have redemption through his blood, even the forgiveness of sins:

Who is the image of the invisible God, the firstborn of every creature:

For by him were all things created, that are in heaven, and that are in earth, visible and invisible, whether they be thrones, or dominions, or principalities, or powers: all things were created by him, and for him:

And he is before all things, and by him all things consist.

And he is the head of the body, the church: who is the beginning, the firstborn from the dead; that in all things he might have the preeminence.

For it pleased the Father that in him should all fulness dwell;

And, having made peace through the blood of his cross, by him to reconcile all things unto himself; by him, I say, whether they be things in earth, or things in heaven.

1 Timothy 2:1-8
I exhort therefore, that, first of all, supplications, prayers, intercessions, and giving of thanks, be made for all men;

For kings, and for all that are in authority; that we may lead a quiet and peaceable life in all godliness and honesty.
For this is good and acceptable in the sight of God our Saviour;

Who will have all men to be saved, and to come unto the knowledge of the truth.

For there is one God, and one mediator between God and men, the man Christ Jesus;

Who gave himself a ransom for all, to be testified in due time.

Whereunto I am ordained a preacher, and an apostle, (I speak the truth in Christ, and lie not;) a teacher of the Gentiles in faith and verity.

I will therefore that men pray everywhere, lifting up holy hands, without wrath and doubting.

Hebrews 10:4-12
For it is not possible that the blood of bulls and of goats should take away sins.

Wherefore when he cometh into the world, he saith, Sacrifice and offering thou wouldest not, but a body hast thou prepared me:

In burnt offerings and sacrifices for sin thou hast had no pleasure.
Then said I, Lo, I come (in the volume of the book it is written of me,) to do thy will, O God.

Above when he said, Sacrifice and offering and burnt offerings and offering for sin thou wouldest not, neither hadst pleasure therein; which are offered by the law;

Then said he, Lo, I come to do thy will, O God. He taketh away the first, that he may establish the second.

By the which will we are sanctified through the offering of the body of Jesus Christ once for all.

And every priest standeth daily ministering and offering oftentimes the same sacrifices, which can never take away sins:

But this man, after he had offered one sacrifice for sins forever, sat down on the right hand of God;

James 1:12-17
Blessed is the man that endureth temptation: for when he is tried, he shall receive the crown of life, which the Lord hath promised to them that love him.

Let no man say when he is tempted, I am tempted of God: for God cannot be tempted with evil, neither tempteth he any man:

But every man is tempted, when he is drawn away of his own lust, and enticed.

Then when lust hath conceived, it bringeth forth sin: and sin, when it is finished, bringeth forth death.

Do not err, my beloved brethren.

Every good gift and every perfect gift is from above, and cometh down from the Father of lights, with whom is no variableness, neither shadow of turning.

1 Peter 2:4-10
To whom coming, as unto a living stone, disallowed indeed of men, but chosen of God, and precious,

Ye also, as lively stones, are built up a spiritual house, an holy priesthood, to offer up spiritual sacrifices, acceptable to God by Jesus Christ.

Wherefore also it is contained in the scripture, Behold, I lay in Sion a chief corner stone, elect, precious: and he that believeth on him shall not be confounded.

Unto you therefore which believe he is precious: but unto them which be disobedient, the stone which the builders disallowed, the same is made the head of the corner,

And a stone of stumbling, and a rock of offence, even to them which stumble at the word, being disobedient: whereunto also they were appointed.

But ye are a chosen generation, a royal priesthood, an holy nation, a peculiar people; that ye should shew forth the praises of him who hath called you out of darkness into his marvelous light;

Which in time past were not a people, but are now the people of God: which had not obtained mercy, but now have obtained mercy.

1 John 3:3-11
Behold, what manner of love the Father hath bestowed upon us, that we should be called the sons of God: therefore the world knoweth us not, because it knew him not.

Beloved, now are we the sons of God, and it doth not yet appear what we shall be: but we know that, when he shall appear, we shall be like him; for we shall see him as he is.
And every man that hath this hope in him purifieth himself, even as he is pure.

Whosoever committeth sin transgresseth also the law: for sin is the transgression of the law.

And ye know that he was manifested to take away our sins; and in him is no sin.

Whosoever abideth in him sinneth not: whosoever sinneth hath not seen him, neither known him.

Little children, let no man deceive you: he that doeth righteousness is righteous, even as he is righteous.

He that committeth sin is of the devil; for the devil sinneth from the beginning. For this purpose the Son of God was manifested, that he might destroy the works of the devil.

Whosoever is born of God doth not commit sin; for his seed remaineth in him: and he cannot sin, because he is born of God.

In this the children of God are manifest, and the children of the devil: whosoever doeth not righteousness is not of God, neither he that loveth not his brother.

For this is the message that ye heard from the beginning, that we should love one another.

Revelation 1:3-8
Blessed is he that readeth, and they that hear the words of this prophecy, and keep those things which are written therein: for the time is at hand.

John to the seven churches which are in Asia: Grace be unto you, and peace, from him which is, and which was, and which is to come; and from the seven Spirits which are before his throne;

And from Jesus Christ, who is the faithful witness, and the first begotten of the dead, and the prince of the kings of the earth. Unto him that loved us, and washed us from our sins in his own blood,

And hath made us kings and priests unto God and his Father; to him be glory and dominion for ever and ever. Amen.

Behold, he cometh with clouds; and every eye shall see him, and they also which pierced him: and all kindreds of the earth shall wail because of him. Even so, Amen.

I am Alpha and Omega, the beginning and the ending, saith the Lord, which is, and which was, and which is to come, the Almighty.

Revelation 5:1-14

And I saw in the right hand of him that sat on the throne a book written within and on the backside, sealed with seven seals.

And I saw a strong angel proclaiming with a loud voice, Who is worthy to open the book, and to loose the seals thereof?

And no man in heaven, nor in earth, neither under the earth, was able to open the book, neither to look thereon.

And I wept much, because no man was found worthy to open and to read the book, neither to look thereon.

And one of the elders saith unto me, Weep not: behold, the Lion of the tribe of Judah, the Root of David, hath prevailed to open the book, and to loose the seven seals thereof.

And I beheld, and, lo, in the midst of the throne and of the four beasts, and in the midst of the elders, stood a Lamb as it had been slain, having seven horns and seven eyes, which are the seven Spirits of God sent forth into all the earth.

And he came and took the book out of the right hand of him that sat upon the throne.

And when he had taken the book, the four beasts and four and twenty elders fell down before the Lamb, having every one of them harps, and golden vials full of odours, which are the prayers of saints.

And they sung a new song, saying, Thou art worthy to take the book, and to open the seals thereof: for thou wast slain, and hast redeemed us to God by thy blood out of every kindred, and tongue, and people, and nation;

And hast made us unto our God kings and priests: and we shall reign on the earth.

And I beheld, and I heard the voice of many angels round about the throne and the beasts and the elders: and the number of them was ten thousand times ten thousand, and thousands of thousands;

Saying with a loud voice, Worthy is the Lamb that was slain to receive power, and riches, and wisdom, and strength, and honour, and glory, and blessing.

And every creature which is in heaven, and on the earth, and under the earth, and such as are in the sea, and all that are in them, heard I saying, Blessing, and honour, and glory, and power, be unto him that sitteth upon the throne, and unto the Lamb for ever and ever.

And the four beasts said, Amen. And the four and twenty elders fell down and worshipped him that liveth for ever and ever.

Index of Topics

ADORATION
All Hail the Power of Jesus Name 100
Blessed be the Name 181
Glory to His Name 143
How Great Thou Art 22
To God Be the Glory 146

ADVENT
Joy to the World 251
O Come, All Ye Faithful 251

ASSURANCE
A Child of the King 232
All Thru the Night 28
Blessed Assurance 29
Blessed Quietness 203
Farther Along 203
God Leads Us Along 160
He Brought Me Out 18
He Leadeth Me 202
His Eye Is on the Sparrow 239
I'm Happy with Jesus Alone 180
In Times Like These 92
Jesus Understands 217
Leaning on the Everlasting Arms 245
Master, the Tempest Is Raging 247
Never Alone 248
Now I'm Saved 182
The Lily of the Valley 30
The Solid Rock 13

ATONEMENT
At the Cross 84
I See A Crimson Stream 35

Nothing But the Blood 36
Thank God for the Blood 39
What a Wonderful Savior 46

BENEDICTION
God Be With You 257

BLESSING
Count Your Blessing 141
Even Me 234
More Abundantly 173
There Shall Be Showers of Blessing 47

CARE
Does Jesus Care 50
God Will Take Care of You 51
Jesus Understands 217

CHURCH, BODY OF CHRIST
A Glorious Church 205
Baptized into the Body 54

COMFORT
Blessed Quietness 202
God Leads Us Along 160
I Must Tell Jesus 187
Leave It There 52
The Beautiful Garden of Prayer 60
The Haven of Rest 196
The Storm is Passing Over 12
What a Friend We Have in Jesus 61

COMMITMENT
I Am Going On With Jesus 62
I Am Out on the Battlefield 284
I Surrender All 63
I'd Rather Have Jesus 126

Jesus Is Calling..65
Never Draw Back 277
Nothing Between 67
Where He Leads Me 69

CONFIDENCE
I've Anchored in Jesus 58
Leaning on the Everlasting Arms 245
The Lily of the Valley 30
Tis So Sweet to Trust in Jesus................................. 147

CONSECRATION
Deeper, Deeper 1
Fill Me Now...80
Give Me a Clean Heart.. 259
His Way with Thee 76
Is Your All on the Altar 72

CREATION
How Great Thou Art 22

DECISION
I Surrender All..63
I'm Going Through 243
Never Draw Back 277

DELIVERANCE
I Will Make the Darkness Light....................................11
Jesus Breaks Every Fetter 59

DISCIPLESHIP
Draw Me, Dear Jesus... 170
Footprints of Jesus... 211
If Jesus Goes With Me 26
Leaving All to Follow Jesus 140
O Master, Let Me Walk with Thee........................ 246
Where He Leads Me 69

ETERNAL LIFE
Face to Face 81
I'll Live On and On 82
On Jordan's Stormy Banks 121
When We All Get to Heaven 112

EVANGELISM
Almost Persuaded 229
Come Unto Me 56
Do You Know Him 176
Don't Turn Him Away 206
Jesus Saves 129
Look and Live 85
Seeking For Me 86
The Way of the Cross Leads Home 220
Throw Out the Life-Line 88

FAITH
Higher Ground 90
I've Believed the True Report 164
My Faith Looks Up to Thee 91
Standing on the Promises 1
Wonderful Peace 215

FELLOWSHIP
Come and Dine 194
Friendship with Jesus 55

GOD'S GREATNESS
How Great Thou Art 22
The Great I Am 156

GRATITUDE
Count Your Blessing 141

GUIDANCE
All the Way My Savior Leads Me 224

Footprints of Jesus 210
God Leads Us Along 160
Guide Me, O Thou Great Jehovah 231
He Leadeth Me 202
His Yoke is Easy 94
Jesus, Savior, Pilot Me 218
In the Service of the King 223
Mountain Railroad 98
Savior, Like a Shepard Lead Us 171
Take the Name of Jesus with You 208

HEAVEN
A New Name in Glory 102
Beulah Land 99
Dwelling in Beulah Land 110
I Feel Like Traveling On 219
I Will to Know 288
I'm Pressing On, On All I Know 290
Just Over in Glory Land 114
O, That Will Be Glory 105
Oh, I Want to See Him 106
The Unclouded Day 122
There's A Highway to Heaven 268
We Will Walk thru the Streets 108
We're Marching to Zion 109
When the Battle's Over 255
When the Roll is Called Up 116
When We All Get to Heaven 112
Won't It Be Wonderful There 113
You Shall Wear a Golden Crown 272

HIS MAJESTY
All Hail the Power of Jesus Power 100
Come, Thou Almighty King 145

HOLINESS
Give Me a Clean Heart 259

Holiness unto the Lord 150
I'm Going to Live the Life I Sing About in My Song 281
More About Jesus 210

HOLY SPIRIT
Baptized into the Body 54
Fill Me Now 80
Since the Comforter Came 166
The Comforter Has Come 152

INVITATION
Almost Persuaded 230
Answer Him Lord I Will 265
Do You Know Him 176
Don't Turn the Savior Away 205
I Love to Tell the Story 83
Jesus Is Calling 65
Just As I am 190
Kneel At the Cross 193
Look to the Lamb of God 225
Softly and Tenderly 66
The Shepard Calling His Sheep 168

JOY
Come, Thou Fount 89
Oh, the Joy That Came to Me 273
O Happy Day 213
In the Service of the King 222
Joy Unspeakable 237

LOVE
I Love Jesus 289
I Love Jesus Best of All 234
Love Lifted Me 188
My Jesus, I Love Thee 133
Oh, How I Love Jesus 71

OBEDIENCE
Trust and Obey 138
Where He Leads Me 69

THE ONENESS OF GOD
All in Him 158
Go On In Jesus Name 167
Jesus, the Son of God...4
Take the Name of Jesus with You 208
The Author and the Finisher... 261
The Great I Am.. 156
The Name of God 154
The Water Way...6
Yes, there is Power in His Name... 278

PATRIOTISM
Battle Hymn of the Republic 233

PEACE
It Is Well With My Soul 185
Wonderful Peace 214

PENTECOST
Since the Comforter Came 166
The Comforter Has Come... 152

PERSEVERANCE
I Am Determined to Hold Out 200

PRAISE
Blessed Be the Name.. 181
By the Rivers of Babylon 148
God Is Great In My Soul.. 144
His Name Should Be Praised..2
I Will Praise Him.. 124
It Is Truly Wonderful 292
Praise Thy Name.. 142

To God Be the Glory 146

PRAYER
All Alone 264
I Need Thee Every Hour 216
I Must Tell Jesus 187
Just A Closer Walk with Thee 95
Just A Little Talk With Jesus 262
Let Jesus Fix It for You 184
Sweet Hour of Prayer 262

PROVISION
Great is Thy Faithfulness 20

PROTECTION
He Hideth My Soul 198
Leaning on the Everlasting Arms 245
Savior, Like a Shepard Lead Us 171

REDEMPTION
I See a Crimson Stream 35
Jesus Paid It All 41

REPENTANCE
If I Were You, I'd Make a Change 290
I'm Going Back to Jesus 270
Whiter Than Snow 74
Your Heart Must Be Clean 183

RESURRECTION
Christ Arose 49
Death Hath No Terror 172
Face to Face 81
He Lives 24
On Jordan's Stormy Banks 121
One Day 118

REVIVAL
Let's Go Back 282
Revive Us Again 189

SALVATION
All That Thrill My Soul 5
He Took My Sins Away 48
I Was Lost 274
I'm So Glad Jesus Lifted Me 290
It Took a Miracle 128
Jesus Paid It All 41
Now, I'm Saved 182
Rock of Ages 17
Saved, Saved 16
Somebody Saved Me 135
There Is Power in the Blood 34
Worthy is the Lamb 174

SPIRITUAL WARFARE
Onward Christian Soldiers 238

TESTIMONY
Blessed Assurance 29
He Brought Me Out 18
He Took My Sins Away 48
Heavenly Sunlight 228
I Can Tell the World About This 279
I Walk With the King 214
I'm So Glad Jesus Lifted Me 289
It Is Truly Wonderful 292
Jesus Is All the World to Me 70
Jesus, I'll Never Forget 265
Let the Redeemed Say So 178
Love Lifted Me 188
O Happy Day 213
Oh, What's He Done for Me 275
Since Jesus Came into My Heart 258

Sweeter as the Years Go By 221
That is Why I'm Going to Continue 241
What He Done For Me.. 286
Woke Up this Morning With My.. 227

THE BLOOD OF JESUS
Are You Washed in the Blood... 229
Hide You In the Blood 45
Nothing but the Blood...36
Thank God for the Blood..39
The Blood Prevails...44
There is a Fountain Filled...42
There Is Power in the Blood..34
Under the Blood 38
Washed in the Blood 40
When I See the Blood 37

THE CROSS
Alone... 226
At Calvary..43
At the Cross..84
Glory to His Name.. 143
He Was Nailed to the Cross 192
I See a Crimson Stream..35
Lead Me to Calvary.. 186
Near the Cross... 191
The Cross Is Not Greater...33
The Old Rugged Cross... 253

THE SECOND COMING
Caught Up to Meet Him.. 270
One Day 118
The Day of Redemption 10
When the Roll is Called Up Yonder....................................... 116

THE WORD OF GOD
Deeper, Deeper..1

In Times Like These 92
It Took A Miracle 128
More About Jesus 209
Standing on the Promises 14

TRIALS
Farther Along 204
It Is Well With My Soul 185
Leave It There 52
Never Alone 249
The Storm Is Passing Over 12
We'll Understand It Better By 8

TRUST
Jesus, Lover of My Soul 137
Leaning on the Everlasting Arms 245
My Father Watches Over Me 130
Tis So Sweet to Trust in Jesus 147
Trust and Obey 138
Trusting Jesus 139
We Have an Anchor 207

Index of First Lines

A friend of Jesus, Oh what bliss 55
A wonderful Savior is Jesus my Lord 198
Alas and did my Savior bleed 84
All hail the power of Jesus' name 100
All praise to Him who reigns above 180
All that thrills my soul is Jesus 5
All the way My Savior leads me 224
All to Jesus I surrender 63
Almost persuaded now to believe 230
Am I a soldier of the cross 255
Are you in the Church triumphant 54
Are you trusting Jesus, All along the way 173
As I journey through the land 106
As we fight life's rugged battles 169

Be not dismayed whatever be-tide 51
Blessed Assurance, Jesus is mine 29
Blessed Jesus, Thou hast saved me 142
Bow'd beneath your burden, is there none to share 217
By and by, when the morning comes 197

Called unto to holiness, Church of out God 150
Christ has for sin atonement made 46
Christ our Redeemer died on the cross 37
Come from the loathe-some way of sin 45
Come By here good Lord come by here 288
Come Unto Me 56
Come, Thou almighty King, Help us thy name to sing 145
Come, Thou Fount of every blessing 89
Come, we that love the Lord 109

Death has no terrors for the blood brought one 172
Deeper, deeper in the love of Jesus Daily let me go 1
Do you hear them coming brother 205
Do you know Jesus, our Lord, our Savior 4

Does Jesus care when my heart is pained 50
Down at the cross where my Savior died 143
Down in the valley where the violets grow 280
Draw me, dear Jesus, draw me Nearer unto thee 170

Every day, everywhere on the busy thoroughfare 281

Face to Face with Christ my Savior 81
Far away in the depths of my spirit 215
Far away the noise of strife upon my ear is falling 110

Give me a clean heart so I may serve Thee 259
God be with you till we meet again 257
God is Elohim of all the holy prophets 158
God shall be first in everything 276
God's greatness is seen, In the Heaven above 144
Great is Thy faithfulness, O God my Father 20
Guide me, O Thou great Jehovah 231

Have thy affections been nailed to the cross 68
Have you been to Jesus for the cleansing power 229
He leadeth me, O blessed thought 202
He pardoned my transgressions 291
He sanctified me with the Holy Ghost 285
He's on the mountain calling His sheep 168
He's the Author and the Finisher 261
He's the great I am 156
Hear the blessed Savior calling the oppressed 58
Hover other me, Holy Spirit 80

I am going on with Jesus 62
I Am Determined To Hold Out 200
I am happy in the service of the King 223
I am now on the altar 59
I am Thine, O Lord, I have heard thy voice 76
I am weak, but Thou art strong 95
I believe every word of God 241

I came to Jesus, weary, worn, and sad 48
I can hear my Savior calling 69
I can tell the world this 278
I have found a friend in Jesus, He's everything to me 30
I have found His grace is all complete 237
I have found the God of Israel 2
I hear the Savior say, Thy strength indeed is small 41
I heard the voice of Jesus say, Come unto Me and rest 30
I know a man, from Galilee 176
I love Jesus, So do I 289
I love to sing and pray, rejoicing every day 234
I love to tell the story of unseen things above 83
I must needs go home by the way of the cross 220
I must tell Jesus all my trails 187
I need Jesus, my need I now confess 78
I need Thee every hour, most gracious Lord 216
I once was lost in sin but Jesus took me in 262
I rejoice in my Savior's love today 44
I serve a risen Savior, He's in the world today 24
I trust in God wherever I may be 130
I was one a sinner 104
I was alone and idle. I was a sinner too 283
I will make the darkness light before thee 11
I will to know if He will welcome me there 288
I'd rather have Jesus than silver or gold 126
I'm going back to Jesus, I can no longer wander 271
I'm pressing on the upward way 90
I'm pressing on, on all I know 290
I'm rejoicing now in Jesus 153
I'm so glad, Jesus lifted me 289
I've a home prepared where the saints abide 114
I've a message from Lord 85
I've believed the true report, Hallelujah to the Lamb 164
I've found a Friend who is all to me 16
I've reached the land of corn and wine 99
I've seen the lighting flashing 249
If He's a friend that's true and kind 178

If I walk in the pathway of duty..96
If I were you, I'd make a change 291
If the world from you withhold o its silver and gold 52
If you from sin are longing to be free...................................... 225
If your life in days gone by 184
In loving kindness Jesus came.. 188
In shady, green pastures, so rich and sweet 160
In sin I wandered sore and sad 39
In sorrow I wandered, my spirit oppressed 214
In this modernistic day, we have strayed too far.................. 282
In times like these you need a Savior......................................92
It may be in the valley, where countless dangers hide............26
It was alone the Savior prayed 226

Jesus Christ my Lord will keep me All thru the night............28
Jesus Christ my Savior, He has set me free............................ 174
Jesus has a table spread 194
Jesus is all the world to me 70
Jesus is calling you to the light 264
Jesus is tenderly calling thee home 65
Jesus keep me near the cross... 191
Jesus loves me with unchanging love...................................... 275
Jesus, I'll never forget, when away down in Egypt land...... 266
Jesus, Lover of my soul, Let me to Thy bosom fly.............. 137
Jesus, my Savior to Bethlehem came 86
Jesus, Savior, pilot me, Over life's tempestuous sea............ 218
Joy to the world the Lord is come... 251
Joys are flowing like a river... 203
Just as I am, without one plea 190
Just come on with your money 284

King of my life, I crown thee now 186
Knell at the cross, Christ will meet you there....................... 193

Leaving all to follow Jesus 140
Life is like a mountain railway...98
Long ago the maids drew water In the evening time................6

Lord I hear of showers of blessing 235
Lord Jesus, I long to be perfectly whole 74
Lord, I have started to walk in the light 243
Lord, keep my soul from day to day 38
Low in the grave He lay, Jesus my Savior 49

Master, the tempest is raging 247
Mine eyes have seen the glory 233
More about Jesus I would know 210
My faith looks up to thee 91
My Father is omnipotent and that you can't deny 128
My Father is rich in houses and lands 232
My heart was distressed 'neath Jehovah's dread frown 18
My heavenly home is bright and fair 219
My hope is built on nothing less than 13
My Jesus, I love thee 133
My soul in sad exile was out on life's sea 196
My way gets brighter 267

No confusion up there in My Father's house 286
Nothing between my soul and the Savior 67

O come, all ye faithful, joyful and triumphant 252
O courage, my soul, and let us journey on 12
O Happy day that fixed my choice On Thee 213
O I woke up this morning with my mind 227
O Lord my God! When I in awesome wonder 22
O Master, let me walk with Thee 246
O spread the tidings round wherever man is found 152
O they tell me of a home far beyond the skies 122
Of Jesus love that sought me 221
Oh glory to the Lord, all my sins He took away 273
On a hill far away stood an old rugged cross 253
On Calvary's hill of sorrow 35
On Jordan's stormy banks, I stand 121
On Mt. Olive's sacred brow 263
On the great day that's coming to all 183

Once I was far from Jesus my life was filled with sin 182
One day I'm going where Jesus is 269
One day when heaven was filled with His praises 118
Onward, Christian soldiers, Marching as to war 238

Pass me not gentle Savior, Hear my humble cry 134

Rock of Ages, cleft for me, Let me hide myself in Thee 17

Savior, like a shepherd lead us 171
Shadows may gather and strong clouds may roll 268
Simply trusting every day 139
Since Christ my soul from sin set free 104
Sing the wondrous love of Jesus 112
Softly and tenderly Jesus is calling 66
Some people wonder why we say 266
Somebody sought me when I was wandering 135
Soon this life will all be over 101
Standing on the promises of Christ my King 14
Sweet hour of prayer 262

Take the name of Jesus with you 208
Tempted and tried we're oft made to wonder 204
The cross that He gave may be heavy 33
The Lord is my shepherd 94
The mighty God is Jesus 158
The name of Jesus is so sweet 136
The nations are breaking, And Israel's awaking 10
The Savior is calling, is calling for you 206
The service of Jesus true pleasure affords 123
The test is on everywhere I go 274
There have been names that I have loved to hear 132
There is a fountain filled with blood 42
There is a Name I love to hear 71
There is coming a day when to judgement we must 87
There is something mighty sweet about the Lord 290
There shall be showers of blessing 47

There's a garden where Jesus is waiting....................................60
There's a secret God has hidden 154
There's not a friend like the lowly Jesus 64
There's nothing so precious as Jesus to me 180
They led to Bethany, there's where He stayed..................... 211
Throw out the Life-Line across the dark wave......................88
Time is filled with swift transition... 120
Tis a sweet and glorious thought comes to me 82
Tis so sweet to trust in Jesus 147
To God be the glory great things He hath done.................. 146

Upon life's boundless ocean where mighty billows roll.........58

Walk with Me Lord, Walk With Me....................................... 288
Walking in sunlight, all of my journey 228
Washed in the blood, by the Spirit sealed 40
Watch ye therefore ye know not the day.............................. 271
We are often tossed and driven 8
We have heard the joyful sound 129
We now walk thru the valley and shadow........................... 108
We praise Thee, O God, For the Son of Thy love 189
What a fellowship, what a joy divine.................................... 245
What a friend we have in Jesus 61
What a wonderful change in my life 258
What a wonderful, wonderful Savior..................................... 192
What can wash away my sin 36
What makes the virtue in the water...................................... 277
When all my labors and trails are over................................. 105
When I first found Jesus.. 200
When I saw the cleansing fountain 124
When my life work is ended... 209
When my Savior found me... 272
When peace like a river attendeth my way 185
When the Lord turned again the captivity of Zion.............. 148
When the trumpet of the Lord shall sound 116
When upon life's billows you are tempest tossed 141
When we walk with the Lord in Light of His Word............ 138

When with the Savior we enter the glory land 113
Who can cheer the heart like Jesus 5
Who healed my wounded heart one evening 279
Why should I feel discouraged 239
Will your anchor hold in the storms of life 207
Would you be free from the burden of sin 34
Would you live for Jesus 76

Years I spent in vanity and pride 43
Yesterday, today, forever, Jesus is the same 161
Yield not to temptation, for yielding is sin 161
You have longed for sweet peace and faith increase 72

Index of Authors and Composers

Abbey, M. E.	98
Ackley, Alfred H.	24, 223
Acuff, James W	114
Alwood, J. K.	122
Baker, Mary A.	247
Baring-Gould, Sabine	238
Baxter, Lydia O	208
Bennard, George	253
Black, James M.	116
Blandy, Ernest W	69
Bliss, Philip P	230
Boberg, Carl	22
Bonar, Horatius	32
Booker, Melvia	28
Booth, Ballington	33
Bottome, Frank	152
Bradbury, William B.	13
Budd, Ida M.	140
Buell, Harriet E	232
Buffum, Herbert	243
Butler, Charles J	104
Byrd, G. T.	263
Campbell, Lucie E.	211
Carter, Russell K.	14
Chapman, Wilbur J.	118
Childs, A. A.	87
Chisholm, Thomas O.	20
Clark, F. A.	8
Clark, Harry D.	206
Clark, William H.	180
Codner, Elizabeth H.	235
Cornelius, Rufus H.	106
Cornell, Warren D.	215

Cowper, William 42
Crosby, Fannie J. 29, 65, 75, 134, 191, 198, 209, 224

Derricks, Lister C. 262
DeVenter, Van Judson 63
Doddridge, Philip 213
Douroux, Margaret J. 259

Elliott, Charlotte 190
Ellor, James 100

Farrow, George R. 158
Featherston, William R. 133
Ferguson, Manie P. 203
Foote, John G. 37
Ford, H. J. 135
Fry, Charles W. 30

Gabriel, Charles H. 79, 105, 130, 188
Gilmore, Joseph H. 194
Gilmour, Henry L. 18, 196
Gladden, Washington 246
Graeff, Frank E. 50
Graves, Frederick A. 192
Grimes, S. K. 156, 166

Hall, Elvina M. 41
Hamilton, C. S. 200
Hamilton, T. P. 200
Hankey, Katherine A. 83
Harewood, Gladstone T. 44, 170, 182, 234
Harris, Margaret J. 48, 124
Harris, Thoro 5, 172
Hastings, Thomas 16
Hasty, E. E. 86
Hawks, Annie S. 216
Hays, William S. 30

Haywood, Garfield T. 4, 10, 35, 39, 54, 108, 154
Hewitt, Eliza E. 38, 112, 210
Hoffman, Elisha A................................. 46, 68 72, 143, 187, 245
Hopper, Edward 218
Hine, Stuart...22
Hudson, Ralph E. 94, 205
Huston, Frank C. 123
Hussey, Jennie 186

Jackson, Henry G.. 225
Jones, Charles P.........................1, 11, 34, 40, 56, 165, 172, 180
Jones, Lewis E. 34
Jones, Ruth C. 93

Kirkpatrick, William J..147, 152

Laney, Thomas J. 82
Lawson, Robert C. 3, 142, 144, 148, 167, 174, 178
Lowry, Robert..36, 49, 60
Ludgate, Joseph C...55

Mackay, J. B. 189
Marks, William E...97
Marsh, Charles H. 119
Martin, Civilla D.. 51, 240
Martin, W. C. 131, 136
McDaniel, Rufus H.. 258
Miles, Charles A 27, 103, 111
Miller, Rhea F. 127
Miller, William 219
Moody, Charles E. 193
Morris, Lelia N. 151, 222

Newell, William R 43
Nicholson, James 74
Nusbaum, Cyrus S. 77
Oatman, Johnson 64, 90, 97, 141

Ogden, William A. 85
Owens, Priscilla 129, 207

Palmer, Horatio R. 91, 163, 248
Parker, Mary Lou 177
Perronet, Edward 101
Peterson, John W 128
Pickett, Ludie B 249
Pounds, Jessie B. 220
Pryor, Hattie 3, 7

Robinson, Robert 89
Rowe, James 113, 214

Sammis, John H. 138
Schooler, A. R. 183, 261
Scriven, Joseph P. 61
Snow, Eliza R. 98
Spafford, Horatio G 185
Stead, Louisa R. 147
Stennett, Samuel 121
Stevens, W. B. 204
Stites, Edgar P. 99, 139
Stokes, Elwood R. 80

Tessier, Albert D 260
Thompson, Will L. 66, 70
Thrupp, Dorothy A 171
Tindley, Charles A. 9, 12, 52, 67, 184
Toplady, Augustus M. 17
Tomer, William G 257
Tullar, Grant C. 81

Ufford, Edward S. 88

Wade, John F. 252
Walford, William W. 57

Warren, Barney E. 237, 291
Watts, Isaac 84, 109, 251, 255
Webster, George O. 79
Weeden, Winfield S. 63
Wesley, Charles 137, 145
Whitfield, Frederick 71
Whittle, Daniel W. 47
Williams, William 231
Wilson, Jennie 120, 264

Young, George A. 161

Zelley, Henry J. 19, 228

400

Acknowledgments

All That Thrills My Soul © 1931, renewed 1959 and this arr. 2000 Nazarene Publishing House (admin. by Music Services) All Rights Reserved. SESAC.

Sweeter as the Years Go By © 1970, renewed 1998 Lillenas Publishing Company (admin. by Music Services) All Rights Reserved. SESAC.

How Great Thou Art © 1986 Lillenas Publishing Company (admin. by Music Services) All Rights Reserved. SESAC.

A New Name in Glory © 1987 Southern Faith Songs (admin. by Music Services) All Rights Reserved. BMI.

Come Unto Me © 1965, renewed 1993 Lillenas Publishing Company (admin. by Music Services) All Rights Reserved. SESAC.

About the Editor

Apostle Cornelius Showell was called into the Kingdom for such a time as this as a man destined to empower the masses through his prolific preaching and teaching. His passion for the Kingdom and the things of God and compassion for men and women's souls have made him sought after to preach good tidings proclaim liberty to the meek and captive.

After receiving the mantle from his father, the Honorable Bishop Winfield Amos Showell, in 1987, he became the senior pastor of, one of the oldest Apostolic churches in the United States, The First Apostolic Faith Church of Jesus Christ, International in Baltimore.

A noted Baltimore entrepreneur and businessman, for over 30 years, Showell has been involved in various real estate and commercial endeavors as a manager, developer, and owner. In keeping with his noted care for the senior citizens of Baltimore, his ventures include the development of two multi-unit housing complexes for the elderly.

A scholar of African American history, he was the founding executive director of the Maryland Commission on Negro History and Culture, taught African American Studies at Morgan State University for numerous years, and was instrumental in establishing AFRAM, Baltimore City's highly acclaimed African American Heritage Festival.

In 2002, Showell was consecrated to the Apostleship by the Executive Board of Bishops of the Bible Way Church of our Lord Jesus Christ, Incorporated. He served as Presiding Bishop and Chief Apostle of International Bible Way Church of Jesus Christ, Inc. from 2006-2014. As such he provided guidance to over 500 pastors and several affiliate organizations heads through his wisdom and leadership.

Apostle Showell is married to the love of his life, the Elect Lady Augusta Showell. They have three sons, Byron, Andre, and Cornelius, II.